Notes from the Sidelines

Notes from the Sidelines

Leslie Anne Miller

iUniverse, Inc.
New York   Bloomington

Notes from the Sidelines

iUniverse books may be ordered through booksellers or by contacting:

iUniverse
1663 Liberty Drive
Bloomington, IN 47403
www.iuniverse.com
1-800-Authors (1-800-288-4677)

ISBN: 978-0-595-49256-5 (pbk)
ISBN: 978-1-4401-3100-4 (cloth)
ISBN: 978-0-595-61029-7 (ebk)

Printed in the United States of America

iUniverse rev. date: 12/30/2008

The author is a retired rehabilitation counselor
who began her career as an activity director
in two long-term care facilities from 1975–76
when the author was 24–25 years old.
She is retired due to her own struggle with multiple sclerosis,
and is now a sculptor, painter, and poet.
All persons mentioned by name are real people
the author knew as a young person
who had a lasting impression on the author's life.

Acknowledgments

I want to express my gratitude to the many people who read and listened to my poems and encouraged me to publish, "Notes from the Sidelines."

First on my list has to be my husband, John, who patiently listened to first the ideas, then the first drafts, and finally the finished poems over the course of many years. He always encouraged me to go ahead and publish a book.

I sent sample volumes of my poems to my family and especially appreciate the feedback and encouragement of my Aunt Betty, my most enthusiastic fan. She stated she was getting requests from friends for copies of the poems and thought publishing my poems in a book would be helpful to a lot of people.

Many close friends read and listened to my poems, encouraged me, and provided support that kept me going through the years of writing, editing, and finally completing this book.

One special friend spent a great many hours with the tedious final editing process and to her and her talent, I will be ever grateful.

Contents

Leslie Anne Miller

Today

Stretches lazily before me like a cat
awakening from deep slumber.
Purring with delightful possibilities,
it snuggles against me,
and warms the chill from the night.

It's hungry for experience and meaning,
and it prowls on quiet paw
the many rooms of my spirit.

With feline seductiveness,
it beckons me forth,
unpredictable,
unfathomable,
irresistible,
and unrepeatable.

Today.

May 1998

Suffering Hope

Pain and fatigue plague me.
Tired and discouraged,
my spirit sags,
my confidence slips.
Happiness takes flight.

Life is about making choices
to crumble or create,
to slump or stretch,
to reach behind or beyond.

Each day offers moments
gentle or harsh,
of hush or of haste,
a day to nourish or neglect,
to be in health, or dis-ease,
to soar or to stall.
Life is about making choices.

Though my body can be tethered,
my spirit struggles free.
There is life beyond struggle,
there is the call to be what might be.

I choose hope.
Hope remembers grace.
With hope there is confidence that steadies,
happiness that reassures,
and a spirit that soars like an eagle.

May 1998

Leslie Anne Miller

Cacophony

City lights blaze upward,
blanching away the flickering stars.
Punctuated only by the screech of sirens,
the freeway groans
in its endless monotony of noise.

Surrounded by neon cacophony,
my thoughts clash and grate.
Oh, for the quiet of starlit nights
wrapped in tranquil greenery.
The tumultuous world dissipates
in the silence and peace
of a forested glen.

Yet where is the source of discordant noise?
Does it emanate from the neon screech of the city
or from the inner clang of the discord within?

Harmony is not absorbed from life,
it emerges from inner peace.
Despite outer clamor and distraction,
it is a journey within
to create a wellspring of serenity.

Such a treasure, an inner sanctuary,
a place where life-giving energy can emerge.
Radiating from an inner source,
peace can emerge despite a chaotic world.

Serenity exists in a world of cacophony.

September 1998

The Chasm

Lonely, yet surrounded by people
scurrying about with frenetic busyness,
I ponder the chasm of losses
that separate me from the flurry.
No longer connected
to the rush and gush of work and career,
I am left behind and alone with time.

At first, time was an unfathomable mystery;
what was I to do with time beyond work?
Of what meaning was my time
so often consumed by suffering and pain?

This is the challenge then,
the crowd whizzing past me, and
finding connection and meaning beyond pain.

Ever so slowly, aloneness became solace;
time a wellspring of artistry.
Time is a new place and pleasure,
a poetic and artistic connection
to the maelstrom of people rushing by.

Poetry is an echo of connection across the chasm.

Poetry is an echo of passage across the chasm.

Art is an echo beyond the chasm and beyond time.

November 2002

Leslie Anne Miller

Snowflakes

Snowflakes softy fall
and pause a moment on my window.
Each flake is a unique sparkle
of motion, color, and light.

Every flake radiates beauty
and majesty
in its brief glorious moment in the sun.

We are a bit like snowflakes.
Our life is a moment in eternity.
We can sparkle
with unique motion, color, and light.
Or, we can shadow our sparkle,
creating a wasted lost dribble.

Snowflakes are a grace
at the pleasure of God
to be accepted or ignored.
Our choice is to sparkle
or darken,
to create bwweauty
or a shadow.

Grace is God's pleasure
which creates
each unique light and color.

Ah, to be a beautiful and majestic snowflake

in the grace of God.

May 1998

Anger and Forgiveness

At long last, I have found forgiveness.
The tight knot of my anger
has loosened and freed my spirit.

Forgiveness is a loving comfort,
a soft balm for the soul
emerging from honest thought.

Forgiveness forced is just anger stifled.
It simmers unrequited beneath,
festering an angry boil
threatening to explode its vile.
Anger acknowledged is a wound discovered.
Only out of safety and inner healing
can authentic forgiveness emerge.

I have learned
to listen and honor feelings of anger
as guideposts to wounds that needs healing.
I am grateful for the forgiveness
that arose from the ashes of my anger.

In forgiveness, my spirit is protected and nurtured
and soars with a lightness of being
on the wings of new life.

Forgiveness is anger heard and lessons heeded.

August 1998

Loneliness

Chained to loss,
I am alone,
peering out my window at a world
beyond my reach.
Hours languish into days of longing
for times gone by
when connection and contribution were possible.

My home is a cherished sanctuary and a prison of despair.
I feel alone and forgotten.

Why do I terrify myself with images of abandonment?
Being alone does not, in itself, create loneliness.

Do I not consider myself good company?
Am I alone because I'm afraid to risk anymore?

I can remember that God is my constant companion.
I talk to God as a friend when alone.
I can reach for connection and contribution in new ways.
I can heal in the cherished sanctuary of my home.

With the grace of God, nothing can imprison my soul.
Alone yet not lonely, connected and reaching out,
creating sanctuary and not prison, I am free.
I am nurtured.

I am loved by God.
With God there is no loneliness.

November 2002

The Pivot Point

Loss is a pivot point in life
pointing to gratitude or despair.
Memories ebb with gratitude for capabilities
and grief for capabilities are no more.
Tomorrow anticipated is a source of hope
and also a source of dread.

The capability of the healthy
can be a helping hand or an envied reminder.
Loss provokes compassion and fear.
The perspective at the pivot point,
that of gratitude or that of despair, is destiny.

I can choose the lens through which I view life.

Gratitude loosens the grip of my despair,
for the memories past
and for the hopes of tomorrow.
Loss can transform my life,
making it infinitely more meaningful
than I could ever have hoped,
because I choose gratitude and hope.

Loss is a pivot point in destiny.

November 2002

Leslie Anne Miller

The Grocery Bag

Consider the life of a grocery bag,
folded flat and waiting for use,
finally opened and doubled to play its role,
to carry life's necessities, our food,
in safety until it reaches our homes.

Do people think much about their grocery bags
when they go to the store to buy food,
when they have a basket full of food,
to take home by a dedicated grocery bag
as it fulfills its intended use?

The grocery bag thinks it's important,
because of its vital role,
because it's built for strength,
advertising displayed on its side.
It is, after all, a long journey
from the tree to the pulp to the paper,
from the paper to the handle to the logo,
from the mill to the truck to the store,
where it waits prepared for duty,
from the store to the car to the home.

So the next time you take home a grocery bag,
consider its journey from the tree,
remember its journey to your home,
keeping safe your variety of foods
until it reaches your kitchen table quite full,
to be emptied, then refolded, then reused
for yet another of life's many needs,
ready to carry something to somewhere,
your trusted grocery bag is always there.

March 2003

Bill

Bill dressed in many layers of clothing
as he crept down the hall of the home.
When I saw him I asked, "Where are you going Bill?"
"Well, ah, I'm just going to feed the horses," he'd say.

He walked to his favorite chair where he sat
all day, each and every day.
In the afternoon, I'd walk over and ask,
"How are you doing today, Bill?"
"Well, ah, I'm going to feed the horses," he'd say.
Then a visitor came and sat next to Bill each day.
They did not speak to each other at all.
Bill would glance occasionally at the visitor.
The visitor would smile gently in response.

One day, I approached Bill and the visitor.
"How are you doing today, Bill?" I asked.
Bill glanced at the visitor, then was silent a moment.
"Well, ah, we're going to feed the horses," he said.

I knew then that Bill liked the visitor.
The visitor's presence spoke to Bill.
Their relationship went where words could not take them.
That day I learned to listen to presence and silence.

April 1994

Louie

Louie was a memorable teacher,
paralyzed from the neck down, he couldn't speak.
He taught with his face and his eyes.

A glance at his face and I knew his opinion.
A glance out his window and I knew how much he missed
his days as the chief hunter for his village.
A smile lit up his face and gave sunshine to my day.

Louie taught me that everyone was my teacher.
Louie taught me everything was my teacher.
Louie taught me every moment was my teacher.
Children teach me imagination and growth.
Adults teach me responsibility and love.
The dying teach me hope, and the value of life well lived.
My thoughts teach me who I am and who I can be.

I want to teach love.
I want to teach grace and prayer.
I want teach awareness that teachers are everywhere,
and can teach lessons about who they are,
and what it is that gives their lives meaning,
of what it is that now challenges their lives,
of what they love and where they find love,
of what they hope and where they find hope,
of where they've found the fortitude to live.

Louie was, perhaps, my best teacher.
He was able to speak without words.
A smile from Louie was a moment of sunshine.
A moment of sunshine was a smile from Louie.
All these decades later, I am able to speak
to Louie without needing to use words.
Thank you, Louie, I'll try to pass that on.

December 2002

Old Sweaters

Such a dilapidated run-down rag, that sweater,
worn out, threadbare and scruffy,
tatty and frazzled with age.

Yet, how gingerly he lifted his old sweater,
caressing the shredded memory of youth long past
when it warmed his boyhood college days.
He announced to anyone caring to know
the aged fineness of sweater remembrance.

How fortunate I am for the enduring love
of this steadfast man
who loves old sweaters to antiquity,
proud to cherish their age and memory.

Beyond youth and capability,
when we are wizened and frayed,
old sweaters of timeworn remembrance,
together we will cherish our aged finery
and our love will be adorned in perpetuity,
the enduring love of two old sweaters.

June 1997

Leslie Anne Miller

Let It Be

When I struggle against things
that can't be changed,
I am exhausted, frustrated,
discouraged, and depleted.

With the acceptance
of what can't be changed,
there is grief and pain,
sadness and loss.
Losses piled upon losses
can be overwhelming.

Life is about making choices.

When I accept the things
I cannot change in my life
and "let it be,"
I also have to acknowledge loss.
But loss can be grieved a bit at a time
one hour and one day at a time.

Taking life as it passes,
changing what can be changed,
and accepting what can't,
leaves more energy
to learn and to love,
to celebrate the joys of life.

Grace helps me understand loss
and deepens my appreciation of joy.

Life is about making choices.
I choose to let it be.
I choose to let grace transform loss.

June 2000

Remembering Children

Children can be our teachers.
They watch us intently and engage life with zest.
They reach to touch and feel, taste and smell.
They listen to bells and rattles, barks and meows,
sirens and voices and the quiet.

They mimic and explore.
They squeal and giggle. They cry and wiggle.
They crawl and toddle along.
They grapple and learn. They fail and fall.
They try and try again and again.
They explore life with their whole being,
one moment at a time, one hour at a time
and one day at a time.

Losses can steal from us.
Sight dims. Sound muffles. Smell dulls.
Taste flattens. Touch numbs. Memory lapses.
Movement slows or stops.

So what to do?
Remember children.
Watch the children. Listen to children.
Hold the children. Learn from children.
Children teach joy. Children teach discovery.
Children teach zest for life.

If they squeal and giggle
in delight from a stroller,
it is possible from a wheelchair.
We can crawl and toddle, grapple and learn,
fail and try again and again.

Remember children create possibility,
one moment at a time, one hour at a time
and one day at a time.

So can we.

March 2000

Leslie Anne Miller

Gray Sky

Dark clouds loom
above the blustering wind and rain,
casting lead shadows across the day,
a reminder of the darkness
that stormed into my life.

Turbulent squalls are but one expression
of nature's complexity and magnificence.
Each season and each dawn bring change.

There have been many seasons
and many dawns in my journey;
many days overcast with pain
and fewer days of relaxing ease.

Change offers hope
that a sunny sky exists
beyond gray lead clouds.
A moment of sunshine
always brings with it
a moment of hope.

Hope exists beyond suffering.
Always.

God is the Creator of the dawn
and the seasons and hope.

Hope that always exists
beyond the blustery gray clouds.
Hope for sunlight that always peeks through
and always warms the spirit.
Always, it is hope from God,
and one way he gives us love.

God is love that hopes.

March 2000

Day by Day

Life with losses is a journey
of moment by moment
and day by day life changes.
Comparing my life with others
leaves me disheartened,
pensive, and very sad.

When I take a moment to pause,
I realize every life has losses
with moment by moment
and day by day life changes.
Losses are part of the thread and stitch
in the fabric of my life.
No matter the losses and life changes,
with resolve and faith, we
can create a new direction
of pattern and substance for our lives.

I trust in the direction
of the thread and stitch,
pattern and substance
despite the losses in my life
because in love and prayer,
by the grace of God,
there is always hope,
moment by moment
and day by day.

Contemplating possibilities
within life's limitations
with God always at my side
keeps me hopeful of new life.

God knows the thread and stitch,
pattern and substance,
loss and possibility of life
and He awaits our
love and prayer
to give us hope.

June 2000

Leslie Anne Miller

Cindy

Cindy groped and stumbled from wall to wall,
off balance with swerves and falls
until finally she reached her wheelchair.
She was wizen with age, sharp angled and thin,
often confused with her day and her life.
Cindy possessed no real attraction at all.
She was just an old lady waiting to die,
in a rest home filled with old souls.

Why then, you ask, is she remembered today,
now that almost three decades have passed?
Because any courtesy she received, she always thanked,
with a sincerity that was obvious to all.
It was little things offered that meant much to her,
a lesson in little things remembered.
Today and beyond, she is with me still,
teaching gratitude for little things.

Small things, after all, are the routine of our lives
and they are often taken for granted.
Cindy reminds me today of the gratitude I have
for the little gifts that God bestows.
Small talent, small skill, small smile and word
that connects us all in ways yet unknown.

The memory of Cindy lives with me today
as she has become a part of who I am.
I'm thankful today just to be alive
with the ability to craft a poem.

She'll always be alive in my heart.

November 2002

Anger

Behind my anger lies hurt and fear.
Left unattended,
fears explode and hurt festers.
Anger signals me that there is a need
to better care for myself or others.

I need to allow my feelings to emerge.
This means unlearning what I was taught.

I need my feelings to teach me
the truth about myself and my world.
I need to remember anger is just a feeling
not an action.
Feelings come and then they go.

My feelings are guideposts to my well-being.
Anger can be fuel toward accomplishment.
Anger can teach a need for patience.
or teach a need for healing or safety.
Anger can be a force for what's good.

Feelings come and then they go.
It's how we choose to act that defines us
and defines the life we create.

November 2002

Leslie Anne Miller

Friendship

Friendship is an unfolding gift in life.
It appears unannounced and undeserved,
unexpected and full of possibility
and full of genuine care.

It can easily slip away.
We are busy and rushed,
distracted and preoccupied.
We are so often quite unavailable.

To have a friend is also to be a friend.
It is sharing and giving
and listening to someone's heart.
It takes time.

Friendship is a gift of grace.
It is a grace to be cherished and nurtured,
celebrated and loved.

Friendship is worth pausing for.

Friendship is worth the time.

March 2000

Limitations

Life speaks harshly to me of limitations and losses.
To ignore them would be denial.
I understand these are harsh realities,
real losses and necessary grief.
So I pause a moment to grieve.

Every breath I take,
every step and every thought that
I have is by the grace of God.
And I am still able to breathe deeply
and ponder and celebrate His grace.
So I pause a moment to reflect.

I have all of the life I have been given.
I have all of the time there is.

I need to grieve unavoidable losses
and I need to celebrate undeserved gifts.

All about me is a celebration
of people and critters,
trees and flowers,
artistry and creation.
These are gifts from God.
I accept them despite limitation and loss.

Thank God for them. And, I do.

March 2000

Leslie Anne Miller

Clutter

Consider the value of clutter.
It hides those things not needed,
it creates artful mosaics of stuff
for us to sink into and relax.

Clutter is an invitation to toss that shirt
on the couch where it doesn't belong.
It was an exhausting day at the office.
Clutter doesn't bellow at you to clean up
and never tells you what to do
like that troublesome boss at the office.

Clutter lures you into its clutches,
entices you to add to its artistry
as mosaics becomes beloved sculptures.

The couch becomes well-rounded
as our stuff feeds its insatiable lure.
The chair becomes a piece of high art
as our stuff is piled upon piles.
And, it's no problem walking carefully
over stuff scattered on the floor.
It makes walking more interesting
so a person never gets bored.

The moral of clutter is this;
for some types of people, it enriches their lives
and the value of clutter is woefully ignored.
The wonder of clutter is much beloved
by discriminating folks that live in it.

March 2003

The Time in Between

I resent the medication and equipment,
the needles and procedures,
the interruptions and intrusions,
the time lost and energy spent.
I resent all that it takes to function.
I want a day off from myself.

Yet, the cost of a day off would be unbearable.
There is no day off from my condition.
There can be no day off from myself.
I have to accept my situation with some grace.
I have to stop being overwhelmed with myself.
Being overwhelmed makes me a miserable self.

I have to focus on the time in between
these interruptions,
the time that is beyond the intrusions.
I need to ask God what He wants of my life.
God has a purpose for this suffering soul.

God knows suffering brings me closer to Him.
He gave us His suffering Son on the cross.
My life, as it is, then, is God's purpose.
I need only listen to His voice always there.
I need only pray that His will be done with my life.
There is time in between these medical demands.
And God knows suffering forces me to listen.

There is time in between for me to listen to Him.
My suffering makes me cling to God.
I need only to listen to His voice
and trust in His meaning for my life.
I need only to ask for His mercy and love
and rest in my trust in His divine mercy.

November 2002

Leslie Anne Miller

Service

Proudly she led me through the clutter
of her apartment to the glass patio door.
Outside were stacks of cardboard boxes
adorned with colorful scraps of shredded cloth.
"It's a cat hotel," she announced brightly,
now the neighborhood's lost kitty cats
have a nice place to stay out of the rain."

It was an unusual community service, a cat hotel,
a unique plan she had conceived of herself
to lavish love upon her soggy feline friends,
a dry respite from their neighborhood travels
and a respite from her terminal illness as well.

She fought her illness with eccentricity,
nurtured by a devoted mate of 40 years,
surrounded with her beloved clutter
and proprietress of a cardboard cat hotel.

She has been gone now for quite awhile.
The cat hotel is maintained by her mate.
Though physically she is no longer with me,
the inspiration of her boundless creativity
will always remain aloft in my memory.
She was a person who was happy with herself
because she sought and found how to serve others,
which included her soggy feline neighbors.

In remembrance of Aunt Margaret.

June 1997

Vulnerability

Coping with disability and loss makes me vulnerable
to harm by people who are insensitive or exploitive.
Sometimes they wear a softened veneer of caring,
but what they care about is their power and control.
When they don't ask, don't listen, and don't change,
they continue to harm those who are vulnerable.
They can feign caring as leverage for advantage.

Now that I have been sheltered in the grace of God,
I have learned ways to protect myself from harm.
I focus and listen to that small Voice within me.
I listen to my fear and hurt for warnings.
I seriously heed the counsel of trusted friends.
I ask for help only from the trustworthy.

With the grace of God,
I have let go of my naïveté
and stopped my wishful thinking
that those with a caring veneer are trustworthy.
Taking time and being more aware,
I can discern true caring
because caring actions match caring words.

Harm because I'm vulnerable is possible to fend off
because with the grace of a caring God, there is love.
Harm is no match for the grace of God.

November 2002

Giving

Disability has claimed what I had to give.
Loss is having nothing more to offer.
A true test of faith for a giving person
is loss that leaves little left to give.

A test of creativity is to find something new
to be able to give to a needy world.
Creativity is a gift arising from within
that is capable of shaping meaning
from what seems dire or very hard;
clay or stone or human suffering.

Loss has claimed my apparent gifts
yet left a depth of gifts to yet discover.
I have time and a home that provides sanctuary.
I am loved and I have love to give.
I can write and contemplate, give and receive.
I have the courage to risk failure.
That in itself is a gift to give.

Out of the barren ashes of my suffering and loss
emerges renewed courage, compassion and love
when I allow the grace of God to shape my life.

Love reflects the grace of God in a suffering life.
It is a radiant light in the darkened world of loss.
I learned that happiness can exist amidst suffering.
God hovers close awaiting love and prayer.
Clinging to God's love lights up my world.
I'm grateful for that love to give to others.
Love is the greatest of gifts to give.

November 2002

Lillian

Coffee in one hand, plastic bag in the other,
and a determined expression on her wizened face,
always accompanied by a longtime trusted friend,
Lillian walked slowly and exited the facility door
to share food with her feathered friends each day.

The more popular she became,
the more pigeons became friends
until the parking lot drew pigeons by the score.
Her friends left white droppings everywhere near
until a loud roar of staff displeasure was heard.
Lillian's feathered friends were car's sworn enemies,
leaving white splatters on their windshields and hoods.

This feathered friendship must stop now,
these enthusiastic splatters must cease
or staff would leave their job for a cleaner car lot.
What's a rest home to do with pressure like that?
Lillian's friends had to go, it was as simple as that.

Her coffee in one hand, newspaper in the other,
and a forlorn expression on her wizened face,
still accompanied everyday by her trusted friend,
Lillian would still walk and exit the facility door
to grieve her feathered friends every day.

Still, I wondered if hidden in that paper she carried,
might be a morsel or two that was quite hidden
which might slip after she exited the facility door
and be quite unnoticed by those staff passing by,
except by a pigeon or two that might still be there,
not many to disturb the cars now clean in the lot,
just a few feathered friends stopping by,
thankful for Lillian's care.

November 2002

Leslie Anne Miller

Echoes

There are echoes in my life:
hello, hello, hello, hello;
love you, love you, love you, love you;
miss you, miss you, miss you, miss you;
yes, yes, yes, yes, yes;
knowing, knowing, knowing, knowing,
hoping, hoping, hoping, hoping;
caring, caring, caring, caring.
Does it matter who starts the echo?
Perhaps it matters only that echoes are in my life.
Grateful, grateful, grateful, grateful,
is a good place to begin and end echoes.

July 2000

Shoes

The life of a shoe is not glamorous,
rather pedestrian if truth be known,
weighted under ponderous feet
attached to those lengthy legs
with a torso big and wide and round,
dangling arms and hands and thumbs,
top a large hefty head
sprouting a mane of unruly chaos.

Such a load for a thin layer of leather,
pounded daily on concrete and wood.
The life of a shoe is quite heavy,
consequential to note as well,
carrying the full weight of a person
toward their destined purpose in life.

Without shoes on,
people might not encounter
that rain and sleet and snow
or be unable to depart houses
or arrive on time at their jobs,
unable to pick up their children
or milk and cookies at the store.

People should know the importance
that their pedestrian shoes possess,
dull, perhaps in need of a polish
yet ever ready and always handy
for a walk wherever, when, and why
a person load decides to tread.
Life today is not possible
without a pair of pedestrian shoes.

November 2002

Leslie Anne Miller

Risk

Life is always a risk,
risk of rejection or reaching out,
risk of falling or reaching high,
risk of growth or something challenging,
risk of discouragement or failing,
risk of faith or devout praying,
risk of joy or rejoicing,
risk of peace or compromise.

Losses amplify risk,
risk of isolation or socializing,
risk of safety or high flying,
risk of friendship or someone disliked,
risk of caring or burden,
risk of love or obligation,
risk of faith or self-love,
risk of connection or loss.

And God knows risk,
risk of bleeding or healing,
risk of healing or hoping,
risk of hoping or possibility,
risk of possibility or dead ends,
risk of life, living well beyond loss.

October 2001

Nostalgia

I have memories of those days
when I was young, capable, and bright.
Perhaps, they were the best days of my life.

Today, in contrast, feels sad and dulled.
I am no longer that capable bright youth.
I grieve the ability to do the things
I used to be able to do.

Nostalgia is very deceptive.
Those happy and exciting moments
of my past are woven
into the tapestry of my life,
side by side with moments
of sadness, pain, and struggle.

Today and tomorrow will have moments
that will also be happy or sad.
They too will be woven into life's tapestry.

Nostalgia steals moments from living life today,
moments appreciating the happy and the beautiful,
moments grieving the sadness and the struggle.
When nostalgia whispers sweet nothings to me,
I need not find my life today lacking.

Today does not have more or less meaning.
It is a different part of the tapestry of my life.
Today, this moment, I want to be fully alive,
experiencing each moment as it unfolds,
whatever each moment brings.
I leave the color, the weave
and meaning of my tapestry
to the God above who I trust.

Leslie Anne Miller

I am in good hands to live a full life,
grateful for a life still unfolding,
grateful for a faith still evolving,
grateful to live those happy and sad,
interesting and dull moments,
discovering new abilities as old abilities fade,
discovering God's plan to bring me home.

October 2001

Bargains

Life is truly a bargain.
Every day I live, someone has died.
Every ability I possess is a gift.
My ability to breathe, think, and feel,
are abilities absolutely not earned.
I show up and there they are.
Life is truly a bargain.

Sometimes my struggle clouds appreciation.
I become focused only on losses,
my pain, suffering, and problems.

Reflecting puts my difficulties in focus.
I gain honest perspective and balance.
I have daily struggles and I have friends and loved ones.
I have pain and I can think, ponder and write.
I have fatigue and I can love, care, and dream.
These are some of gifts I have been given.
Life is truly a bargain.

Life does not owe me abilities.
Life owes me nothing at all.
Life is a gift. Life is a bargain.

Struggling can be cheerful. It's an acquired capability.
It's something I have to give. I can give cheer.
I can offer listening. I can offer my thinking.
I can give my sculpture, painting, and writing.
Struggling celebrating bargains,
what a bargain that truly is.

July 2002

Leslie Anne Miller

Side Effects

Fatigue, pain, vertigo,
pills, injections, inhalers,
stumbling, groping, falling;
all these scream losses and frustration.

Loss must be grieved.
Then it presents opportunity
to consider the silver lining
in loss's dark storm clouds.

Because I struggle,
I am made humble.
Compassion for those
who struggle grows.
Pain develops courage.
Companions on the journey are appreciated.
Needing people develops humility.
Struggle stretches the spirit.
Survival brings gratitude.

Gratitude brings grace.
Grace brings serenity.

All of these are side effects
of a journey with loss.

March 2000

Confidence

Confidence inspires respect and regard.
Hesitancy inspires doubt and silence.
Life is worth living with resolve and confidence,
humility, determination, and perseverance.
Life is worth cultivating humble confidence.

Always, people with confidence are found.
One need only seek and discover and
take a moment to observe and notice.

One needs to find a dream or a belief,
and cultivate the ability to stretch
beyond what we think we can become.
No one is going to carry anyone
to their desired goals in life.

Confidence begins with commitment.
to a journey toward a goal or a dream.
Confidence is inspired by a mentor
and earned with honest hard work.
Confidence builds with determination.

Confidence is not something that is free.
It requires the cost of time and energy.
It is well worth all the effort to cultivate
confidence.

July 2002

Leslie Anne Miller

Dusk

The sun slips into the distant horizon and
brilliant hues of coral stretch across the sky.
The day grows quiet as the hush of dusk descends.

My life now is calmly quiet.
Disability has stilled the noise in life.
As my physical health slips away,
so do brilliant hues of success and achievement.

Within the quiet dusk that I live,
I find the shape and meaning of my life.
Within the dusk is the glow of hope,
of opportunity beyond my disability.

I am learning from the quiet dusk of my life.
When I embrace it, I live by the light in my soul.
In that light, I find the strength and hope
to persevere as I face trials and struggle.
In that light, I find the peace and healing
of my spirit as it grows close to God.
In that light I find the calm and quiet
to trust God in a life beyond the physical
where disability and trials are over
and the brilliant hues of eternity prevail.

I'm learning in the quiet dusk of my life
to find the shape and meaning of my spirit.
Within the dusk is the glow of hope,
of opportunity beyond my disability.
Dusk casts shadows that give way to dawn.

Dusk.

January 1999

Suffering Wisdom

Suffering can breed wisdom,
wisdom bought at a high price,
a price not willingly chosen.

Yet, if suffering can bring
wisdom bought at a high price,
can it be a solace of worth and value?

Some say suffering is redemptive,
the wisdom of a Savior long ago,
joining with the suffering of mankind
with an inspired purpose of forgiveness.

Wisdom has a high price
and it does not come easily
but can give life meaning and worth.
If suffering is its price,
so be it.

Wisdom brings gratitude
that suffering is worthwhile
and has a purpose within.
So be it
by the grace of God.

July 1995

Leslie Anne Miller

Appreciation

Some days it is hard to see beyond my world.
It takes my energy simply to cope.

My world has become small and simple,
quiet and restful, loving and reassuring
despite difficult physical challenges.
This is a new world to me.

There was a time when my world was large and complex,
noisy and stressful, competitive and anxious,
fraught with important mental challenges.
That is an old world to me.

I am alive to appreciate and participate.
It is a simple truth discovered in suffering.

There was a time I thought I was here to participate.
It was a truth in part, but only in part.

Appreciation is where my happiness grew gratitude.
It is the better part of the truth about life.
I am here to appreciate and participate
in gratitude.

An important discovery,
appreciation and participation
in gratitude.
Thank God.
And, I do.

July 1995

Gus

He was a one armed homely old drunk,
sober and living in our elderly rest home.
He'd arrive quite suddenly at the door
and then he would peer quizzically
into our area to see
what activity was happening there.
He'd arrive, stand, and then observe
but not speak or join in,
yet he was as interested in us
as we were in him at the door.

There were usually subtle glances between us,
his glaze interested and ours inviting.
There was a bond of sorts that developed with time,
as Gus peered periodically each day.
We were always aware that we cared for each other
as we could count on those glances every day.

What I learned from Gus was the language of acts,
simple caring in small ways day to day.
It seems that was when connection is made
and little acts then become a tradition,
it matters not how little the act was.

I miss Gus today, the old sober drunk,
arriving and observing each day.
Perhaps he glances today from on high,
he interested and me inviting into my heart.

Perhaps in the noisy busyness of today
with its stresses, pressures, and rush,
a glance or two each day from above
by someone interested in me,
would be a bond worthwhile to keep,
so I do.

Dearest Gus, I miss your quiet glance.

November 2002

Leslie Anne Miller

Laughter

When someone laughs heartily,
their body vibrates with delight.
Joy and happiness bubble up like froth,
infecting people nearby
until everyone is laughing
and no one remembers how it started or why.

Laughter is a healing grace from above.

Laughter can erupt from a cartoon
and explode from a joke.
Laughter can poke fun at struggles
with a touch of irony and wit.
Laughter can soothe the agony of pain,
and connect quite disparate people.
Laughter can create ever more laughter,
and is a valued blessing and gift
that creates a source of endless joy.

Laughter is grace with glee
that can move sad to glad.
It can move sorrow to tomorrow
and soothe fears and tears.
It lightens burdens and uplifts the weary.
It delights babies and might wake up an elder.
It makes a smile of a frown,
and jostles the stuck.
Laughter is a creation of God
that gives continual joy endlessly.

Laughter.

July 2000

Paralysis

Slowly, I sink into the quicksand of disability.
I feel immobilized in a gray cast of concrete.

Desperately, I reach out to grab a hold
of something or someone to stop sinking.
I fear I'm drowning in vulnerability.

I reach out for affirmation. I struggle for hope.
I call out for a hand to hold.
Then someone sees me and I connect.
Secure in the grasp of compassion,
I am no longer alone
and with their assistance,
I can pull myself out.

I will remember the lesson
of the hand that reached out.
I will lend a hand to someone else one day
to pull them from the quicksand of despair.

Together, we can do what neither could do alone.
It's a lesson I need to remember.
Connection overcomes paralysis and fear.

April 1999

Leslie Anne Miller

Patience

Growing up in American culture
did not equip me for developing patience.
A flick of my remote
and I change channels in an instant.
My microwave provides instant meals.
The bank machine provides instant cash.
Computers offer instant communication.
There is instant entertainment, food and intimacy.
I live in a culture of instant gratification.

My disability requires infinite patience.
I wait to take medication and wait for it to take effect.
I wait for bad days to leave and for good days to come.
I wait on the phone to talk to my doctor's nurse.
I wait for my doctor's appointments.
I am learning the acquired habit of patience.

Patience is a teacher that offers many lessons.
I am learning tolerance of my disability's effects.
I am acquiring the habit of flexibility.
I am bending with the changing winds of my condition.
I am learning there is always the hope of possibility.
I am starting to use my inner potential.
I am learning to potentate others.
I am becoming more gentle. I can help gentle others.
I can console myself. I can console others.
Patience is an acquired gift of disability.
Patience is a blessing from above.
It has become a solace for me.
It's also a solace for others.

February 2002

Dislike

I didn't like Martha who chattered
endlessly about herself,
never inquiring about anyone else.
She demanded and ordered and instructed.
People fled the room from Martha.
I thought she was self-centered and presumptuous.

Then I considered why I disliked Martha.
I feared feeling mistreated and used.
Then I realized I was the person who allowed it
or fled and neither gave me peace.

When I dislike someone, I dislike myself.
I didn't like that Martha treated me poorly.
I didn't like that I treated myself poorly
which is the real reason I didn't like Martha.
This realization gave me pause.

Now when Martha talks endlessly about herself,
I listen for a time then excuse myself.
When she demands, commands, and instructs,
she demands and instructs only herself.
And now, I no longer dislike Martha,
and I feel much more at peace with myself.

Disliking someone is disliking myself.
Dislike takes love and listening to recede.
Now I listen to dislike, within and without
and then take a moment of pause,
dislike will give way to love.

Remembering Aunt Martha
November 1999

Leslie Anne Miller

Joking

Joking can speak aspects of disability
in a way that doesn't threaten others.
Joking disarms people's fear about interacting.
Laughter connects before fear can distance.

Joking of things of serious earnest starts within.
It begins by allowing passing feelings
and then allowing grace.
It begins with being open to healing
and moments of new perspective.

Joking about the ironies of being disabled
takes God's healing presence.
Joking about coping and healing inspires.

Joking to cover up feelings of pain
reflects a falseness and discomfort.

Joking begins and ends with coping well.
Joking begins and ends with grace.

God is a God of laughter.
Laughter with things of serious earnest
is needed most of all in life
and is a blessed gift from God.

September 1995

Helen

I noticed her standing in line
waiting for dinner with the other guests.
Despite the aluminum walker she held
and the wrinkled spotted dress
and despite her limited vocabulary
of words not saying what she meant,
it was her eyes that spoke and her gestures too.
We became good friends that first day.
We greeted most days she stood in line,
and with eyes and gestures she spoke
of her dignity and courage in spite of the fact
that she had no words to say what she meant,
and despite of the fact that she stood in line
in a home that wasn't hers
with people sad, old and lost
and staff very busy and stressed.
She had a royal bearing, standing in the line,
her hair always combed and coifed.
Her smile always made her bearing glow.
She was a magnificent woman and soul.

One day she appeared at my office door,
in teary and angry upset,
banging her walker on the floor
and pointing down the hallway of the home,
spouting a flurry of words with no meaning
about something important to know,
about something that really mattered.
It took a time of gesture and grimace
before I discovered what she meant.
Her best friend lived down another hall
and had died three weeks ago,
and to her horror and profound regret,
no one had told her so.
We held and cried with each other
about the agony of grieving so,
with no one to share the agony
of being three weeks late to know.

Helen is with me this day still.
She taught me of closeness and language to know
the meaning of life and connection and soul.
We had a deep connection of mind and spirit.

November 2002

The Kitchen Aide Mix Master

I was looking at my mix master while cooking one day,
the Kitchen Aide heavy duty model
and thinking about the amazing way
it turns disparate ingredients
into beautiful creations of good food.
With its heavy dough hook, it can easily knead
the most fragrant types of bread.

It reminds me of people with a purpose
and a heavy duty sense of importance,
and the amazing focused way,
purpose turns disparate folks
into a team with incredible goals.

Space flight is a wonderful example
of a heavy duty sense of purpose
that takes disparate people of different language
and turns them into a performing team
that turns out incredible advances.

In looking at my mix master one day,
the Kitchen Aide heavy duty model
with the dough hook,
and how it got me thinking about life
and disparate people with a purpose,
and how a team with a purpose
can create amazing things for our world,
I took pause at what a mixer inspired.

If my Kitchen Aide mixer can make bread
and purpose can bring people together,
then what we need are more purposes
that inspire yet more people
to become part of a working team
that creates benefit for a better world.

It's amazing the thoughts a mix master inspires,
this Kitchen Aide heavy duty model
that made fragrant tasty bread one day.
I would never have guessed
that this ordinary kitchen item
could inspire such lofty thoughts
about creating a better world.

March 2003

Hope

Life is abundantly hopeful.
Outside my window is hope of spring,
hope for a blossom to come forth from a bud,
hope for rain to quench a thirsty drought.

People are generally hopeful. They hope that life is good
and hope for a productive job. They hope to managed finances
and hope for good relationships. They hope for excellent health.

Health is abundantly hopeful. Hope for strong flexible muscles
and for resistance to disease. Hope to overcome illness
and hope for return to health.

Disability is abundantly hopeful. Hope to live a productive life
and hope for compassionate doctors. Hope for medicines with relief
and hope for support of family. Hope for a job with benefits
and hope for finding strengths.
Hope for the ability to live well.

Thank God for all this abundant hope.
Hope leads to new possibilities
and leads to new opportunities.
Hope need not be submerged in problems.
Like the phoenix from the ashes,
hope can find the ability to soar.

July 2002

Leslie Anne Miller

Regrets

Regrets can wander about in the heart,
pushed away, pushed aside or in denial.
Regrets have a way of pushing themselves
into exhaustion from the effort of hiding.

It might be a place, it might be a person,
it might be the words that were spoken.
Something, sometime, somehow succeeds
to trip the hidden land mine of regrets.

Regrets can wander about the heart,
pushed away, pushed aside, or in denial.
Once triggered the purulent explosion of feelings
can expose the long festering neglect,
with regrets that flood the tired mind and spirit
and overwhelm any effort to fend them off.

Neglected regrets can storm the heart,
no longer pushed or in denial.
They can overwhelm a person with feelings,
huge tidal waves that batter and crash
against the bulwark of hardened souls.

Regrets can fire about the heart,
damaging the spirit at its core.
Unleashed, unrestrained and unrelenting,
they sear and burn and fry
the heart and soul and folks nearby.

Regrets can wander about in the heart
beckoned close, experienced and soothed.
Regrets can create a stronger heart
that can speak of painful lessons learned.
Forgiven regrets dissipate in time,
leaving a whisper barely heard.

March 2003

Madeline

She was beautiful on her 79th birthday,
adorned in her dignity and grace,
her spirit shining beyond illness.

Our visit came at the end of her journey.
She knew she was very close to death.

Her hands were fragile and cold in my clasp
and there was deep sorrow in her eyes.
My heart wept tears that began to well,
"I hate to see you like this," I said.
She whispered softly, "I'm dying you know."
"I know," I said, having learned by phone,
but "I'm not ready to let you go."

That moment seemed an eternity
with our eyes and hands firmly locked,
our tears were a bridge of understanding
about her suffering and pending death.

She died only eight days later,
quietly awakening from a coma to speak
her sad farewells on the closing stage.

More than the years and days of our relationship,
what lives with power in my memory
is that special long moment we shared
on her 79th and final birthday,
when we merged our sorrowed hearts
in that poignant moment in sad acceptance
of living and dying and saying goodbye.

February 2002

Leslie Anne Miller

Isolation

God knows, I have days that are jagged.
My inclination is to retreat within myself.
I fear I am a burden that no one could want
and sometimes it seems too difficult
to rise above my pain to engage life.

I can slip so easily into isolation.

Yet, I know isolation can be a trap
when all I have is myself.
It is a slide downwards into depression
where my suffering can swallow my abilities
and I can loose all perspective and hope.
I become discouraged in a sorrowed despair.

To counter this steep slide into isolation,
I fight by practicing a view of each day
as an opportunity to love or learn
about God and people and the world.
God can then transform my isolation
into hopeful and healing contemplation.

Contemplation can become prayer
and prayer gives grace to reach out.
God knows the path into isolation
and also the journey to connection
with God and people and the world.

I can trust God and have the security
that my life, as it unfolds, despite pain,
is full of possibility and meaning.

Isolation can be an opportunity for prayer
and with prayer my fears become quiet
because with God, I know I am never alone.
Isolation is dissipated in prayer
and prayer gives me strength to reach out
for the connection that can end isolation.

June 2000

Cookies

I remember the cookies of childhood,
oatmeal and gingerbread and chocolate chip,
fragrant and toasty and hot from the oven.
Delightful to smell and see and taste,
cookies are a favorite memory of childhood.

In addition to cookies, there were the other memories.
I remember my piano teacher and girl scout leader,
fragrant moments of love and fun in my memory,
delightful to contemplate and again experience,
these treasured cookie people of long ago.

These special cookie people from my childhood
gave me role models that shaped good character
and guides on how to expand my world.
They are delightful memories to share with others,
these cherished cookie people of long ago.

Oh, how I would like to be able to thank
these special cookie people of my memories
that delighted and shaped my adulthood,
these forever favorite people from my life.

Today, as I make the cookies of my childhood,
oatmeal and ginger bread and chocolate chip,
fragrant and toasty and hot from the oven,
delightful to smell and to sample,
I pause for a moment, between bites of cookie,
to remember the cookie people of long ago,
cookie memories and treasures from childhood.

March 2003

Leslie Anne Miller

Faye

She walked peg-legged with no feet,
they were lost long ago to frost bite.
She came thumping down the long hallway
like the strong beating drum that she was.
She knew that her appearance was appreciated
as her smile glowed bright with good cheer.
She had a mind with sharp keenness of thought,
filled with stories of Alaska long ago.
Her face was etched in wrinkles well earned
and her eyes were huge in thick glasses.

She was anxious to talk to a keen mind or two,
being surrounded by dimness and loss
for the majority of her long waking hours.

A project was needed to put use to that mind,
which longed for a challenge and more meaning,
so when she was asked, she became editor of the paper
for our elder rest home filled with memories.

And, the stories were waiting to be brought to life
by her keen intelligence, interest, and careful notes.
She was up to the task of creating a paper
that was unique to our folks and their tales.

It became a wondrous feat of accomplishment
her seventeen page first and last edition
that said everything needing to be said,
by folks with something that needed saying.

Faye, with her one issue newspaper,
still reminds me these decades later,
that if something does need to be said,
speaking it once is actually enough,
especially if it is brought to life
by a keen mind and inquiring voice
in a one issue seventeen page paper
that said all of what needed to be said.

November 2002

Politics

Disability can be a political issue.
Courageous people with terrible losses
did crawl up our country's capitol steps
shouting for more access to buildings and life
and "The Americans with Disabilities Act"
was the final congressional result.

I speak with shop keepers and store managers
about the spirit of this disability law
that mandates "reasonable access" to living,
such as allowing access to a restroom
or keeping clear a cluttered store aisle.
I must speak out of necessity
because of my own disability.

I know it would be much easier by far
not to talk about this necessary law.
It requires reserves of energy and focus
as well as time to relate and explain.

There is no keeping out of politics for me
if I'm committed to belong in community.
Insisting on access is a political act and
acting enables me to be in community
and to remember that I really do belong.

God knows, it is really something small,
requesting a path down a cluttered store aisle
or to asking for access to the restroom,
but perhaps in this very small manner
it helps to create a kinder world
for the next person who has a disability
needing access to life and community.

June 2000

Leslie Anne Miller

Help

Help has many facets in which to ponder.

Help can be chocked full of feelings;
guilt needing help, guilt withholding help,
comfort receiving help, comfort giving help,
coping with help, coping without help,
help that is useful, help that is useless,
compassionate help, compassionless help,
sensitive help, insensitive help;
help that is caring, help that is careless.

Help has many varied meanings;
There are helpers and people who need help;
help of one's self, help of others;
help as a burden, help as a gift;
help as demeaning, help as empowering;
help as a bother, help as a privilege;
help that has value, help with no value.

Help has many cultural dimensions;
help as an individual, help as a family,
help as a community,
help as a nation, help that is global.

Help has a definite continuum;
help that is rare, help that is occasional,
help that is regular, help that is often,
help that is constant; help that is always,
help that is not helpful, help that is helpful.

Such a quilt of vast feeling and meaning,
dimension, diversity and continuum.

Help.

October 2001

Prayer

Father Dearest, please hear my quiet soul,
reaching high with all my strength for you.
Jesus sweetest, please hear my quiet call,
reaching high with all my will for you
and with grace and will, following your path
to our Father who gave us His only Son.

My cares, my worries and anxieties are soothed
by reaching out for you.
And more than reaching, taking time to be
simply in the company of you,
finding rest in your eternal home.

My happiness, my joy, my gratitude is heard
by reaching out for you.
And more than that, taking time in gratitude
simply in the company of you,
finding bliss in Your divine presence.

Father Dearest, hear my quiet soul.
Jesus sweetest, hear my quiet call.
Bless me Father, heal me Jesus,
give me the strength to share
with those that journey with me,
the joy, the happiness, the gratitude I feel,
reaching out for You
and finding grace to follow You home.

March 2003

Lilly

She was a tiny Alaska Native woman,
a former missionary so they say.
She was frozen in a pretzel contortion
and spent all of her protracted days in bed.
She was remarkable for her smile
that lit up the room when she grinned,
which she did whenever she was moved
by her nurse's aides who were friends.
It took only a little coaxing by friends,
and then Lilly would begin to sing
her beautiful hymns of along ago
when she was a missionary in small villages.
One day there was a grand entrance
of nineteen people dressed in furs,
all claiming Lilly as a relative whom
they had journeyed a distance to see.

Surrounding her bed was this crowd of folks
and tiny Lilly in the middle grinning wide,
when all of these people began to sing
Lilly's soulful hymns of long ago.
Someone ran to record this event in her room
that was so rare and inspiring to all.

Lilly still lies there in bed as a pretzel
and smiles whenever she is moved,
and now to hear Lilly sweetly sing,
it takes but a button to play that tape
and she is surrounded by singing kin.
Lilly taught me about joy amidst loss
and that a smile can light up someone's life,
that a distant family can have and hold
a special type of bond that can be shared
and captured in one unique meeting
for later memories to continue the joy.
It's a gift I ponder many decades later,
love of family, deep bond, and sweet song.

It takes but a smile and a moment of song
to create joy that can last an eternity,
where sweet Lilly now rests,
her legs straight and strong,
welcoming her family as they come
to surround her in their love and sweet song.

November 2002

Justice

A world of vast despair awaits justice
for children underfed and unclothed,
for tiny street urchins who live homeless,
for the impoverished despair grinding children,
leaving shredded memories for the rest of their life.

Disability also can grind the innocent,
leaving them sidelined with shredded dreams.
Society can crush the disabled in their ignorance,
leaving them outcasts with isolated despair.

Justice demands awareness and response.
Justice demands vigilance and persistence.

So, how do we try to live justice today?
We might help a few kids and some families
forced to live in an impoverished world.
It does not have to be a great justice.
It only takes the beginning of justice.
Small response is a bit of justice in the world.

I fight the injustice of my medical mysteries.
I fight slipping into isolation and despair.
I ask for the justice of reasonable access
to restrooms and grocery store isles.
It is justice to be disabled in community.

A small justice is my justice,
one person at a time,
one day at a time,
perhaps helping some kids and families
in their efforts to find a better life.
I try to create a better world for myself
and to create a better a world for others.

It is but a small justice to help out.

But all justice counts in the end.

October 2001

Splatter

Does it matter if a lot of things splatter?
Nothing is lost, just scattered.
This I mumble to myself
when my hand suddenly jerks,
sending a glass flying high or low,
creating a large scattered splatter.

Does it matter if a lot of things splatter?
Nothing is lost just creatively scattered.
I have learned good lessons from splatter,
patience and tolerance and always the hope
that creating splatter again won't occur,
which is an unrealistic idea on my journey.

Does it really matter if a lot of things splatter?
Nothing is lost just creatively scattered.
Scattered splatter to behold can teach virtue,
such as withholding an angry remark,
learning patience, tolerance, and hope.

Does it really matter if a lot of things splatter?
Nothing is lost just creatively scattered.
So much has been gained creating splatter
that I slowly realize that it doesn't matter,
cleaning up splatter takes just a moment,
splatter can be a relaxation technique
and an opportunity to relax with life,
learning to be easy with each moment.
It's not possible to let splatter spoil our joy
unless we invite it to do so.

March 2003

Leslie Anne Miller

Capacity

The eagle and the swallow are different,
each one has a unique capacity as a bird
and each lives its own distinctive life.

In a similar way, my capacity is now different.
There are many things I no longer can do.
I have a different capacity than others
and thus I live a different kind of life.

The world needs the eagles and swallows.
The world needs the owls and canaries
and creatures of every type and capacity.
Each one makes its own contribution.
Each is integral and a unique part of life.

Changes can happen because of losses.
There might be a change of capacity.
There might be a change in life's path.
Change can result in a very different life.

I am grateful for the capacity I continue to possess
and for my unique type of journey through life.
It's a different capacity and a different kind of life
yet it's unique and capacity is a grace of God.

God creates each precious human, plant, and animal
as a sign of His great love acting in our world.
His capacity encompasses creation
and lasts beyond eternity.
We have all been invited to join His love
and endless capacity that lasts for eternity.

June 1997

Pain

Pain is a dark shadow that hounds me.
It intrudes on my efforts to ignore it.
Its steel vice has a grip on my body
and threatens to pierce my soul.
Fleeing its pursuit is exhausting.
Fighting off its onslaught
leaves me discouraged and worn.

Pain is a despair that must be stopped
before it pierces and diminishes the soul.
So at last, wearied of struggle,
I finally ask for help to quiet the pain.

I've learned to ride pain's crest as it changes,
I ebb with waves of relief that wash over me.
At peace with the pain that wracks my body,
at peace with some relief to quell the pain,
my spirit leaps up joyfully in freedom,
light as a whisper in the wind.

Long after the pain has diminished,
the lightness of spirit remains.
Though pain might again cast dark shadow,
I know there is relief to make it more bearable.
I know that I need to ask for help.
When pain is lessened for a moment,
there's a light in my soul,
a light to explore and to encounter.
It is the light of possibility and hope.
Hope remembers grace is close at hand.
Grace is a soul that is joyfully free and
light as a whisper in the wind.

November 2002

Tapestry

Each thread in a tapestry adds texture
that has shape, color, and design.
Tapestry is a kaleidoscope of threads
that are woven in unique creative artistry.
Stepping back to view such a tapestry,
the threads are invisible in the design
yet each thread is unique and irreplaceable
in the magnificence of the finished piece.

God created me as a unique thread
in His grand tapestry of creation.
Each tiny thread has a unique purpose
to the grand creation of life in each moment.
Without my unique presence and contribution
or my unique donation to this moment,
this majesty of the grand design of life
would be an incomplete creation of God.

We have a valuable and a unique contribution to life.
There is not a creature in the world exactly the same.
God is the Artist of life's tapestry
where everyone is a uniquely precious thread.

November 2002

Painting

Reds and yellows,
blues and greens,
hues and intensities,
textures and tones,
splattered and sponged,
retouched and smeared,
lines and shapes,
brushes and canvas,
time lost and time found.
Ah, the bliss of painting and playing,
feeling and praying with color.

April 2003

Leslie Anne Miller

Happiness

If only I could travel or
if only I could still work.
If only I could dance again or
if only I could sing again
then I think I would be happy.
But that happiness depends upon an "if only" dream.

Happiness reaches out to me every single day.
I could invite happiness in for cookies and tea
or be too distracted or busy to see possibilities
and I pass by an opportunity to experience it.

Happiness is definitely an acquired habit,
often deepened with suffering or sorrow.
Happiness can exist accompanied by suffering.
That too is definitely an acquired habit.

I can practice being happy with each day.
I could take pause a moment or two
and notice the flowers in my garden,
or the sun lighting up my bedroom,
or the music that plays on the radio,
or the tender touch of a caring hand.

These little moments of happiness
are experienced day to day without
an "if only" dream.
These moments of happiness are in the moment now.

Happiness deepened is an experience of God's grace.
Noticing grace is also an acquired habit.

October 2001

Trust

Flowers beckon outside my window,
a collage of colored petals
glistening in the summer rain.
The flowers, nourished by rain,
open their petals to the warmth of sun.

I trust God to provide guidance for my spirit
despite a body wracked by pain and infirmity.
I am nourished by the sun, flowers, raindrops,
beauty, and love that grace my life.

Sometimes it is difficult to change focus
when faced with suffering and loss.
In those moments, I have learned to let go,
to trust in God's compassion,
suffering me, healing me,
loving me, and gracing me.
Knowing the comfort of grace
in moments of suffering and need,
I have learned trust in times of loss.

I trust that I have all the life
I have been given to celebrate God.
That means spending time in prayer
listening to God's gentle nudges
toward purpose, meaning, and joy.
And, finding these, taking time to experience
these gifts that flow through me
that can nourish and love other people
who grace my journey through life.

My life is noticing grace that is with me.
Experiencing trust is God's gift of grace,
and trust is a gift to be celebrated and shared.
Trusting God and the life He gives me
brings me peace and serenity
that are also gifts to be celebrated.

October 2001

Leslie Anne Miller

Gossip

Gossip arises out of boredom,
jealousy, and resentment.
Listening to gossip reinforces
and gives it false validity.
Gossip is the poisonous voice
of the unkind and insecure.

Gossip gushes garbage and hides honesty.
Gossip relishes resentment and stifles serenity.
Gossip corrupts caring and ravages regard.
Gossip trashes trust and honor.

To gossip,
to be gossiped about,
speaks of hurt and pain
that is unheard and invalidated.
Gossip is a poisonous arrow
to the center of a heart of love.

Gossip is a slippery slope
of slime that
I do not want in my life.
I need to be careful not to participate
with a careless remark in an idle moment
lest without thinking I begin to slide
into gossip.

November 2001

Blanche

Huddled in her wheelchair with one arm tucked inward,
moving into the room with one foot cocked outward,
eighty-three year old Blanche would patiently wait
as easels were put up and paint readied for the class.
Blanche always responded to greetings from people
with a smile shyly hesitant and a voice barely heard.

She painted with her good arm, using strong bold stokes.
And, always, after a while, she would become angry
and declaring that her painting was no good anyhow,
she would fling her wet paintbrush aside,
proclaiming loudly to all who could still hear,
"Oh, gee whiz, what's the use of this anyhow?"
It took the instructor's patience and encouragement
to point out where she was painting quite well,
before she was gently coaxed into resuming again.

One day there was an arm wrestling contest
after the painting class finished for the day.
Blanche was well known for her strength
in that strong arm of hers,
which was the only arm that worked.
Everyday that arm lifted her weight several times.
It was a very good arm for a wrestling match.
For fun she took on a mere youngster
of just twenty-five years old.
Folks laid bets on who would win
this match between young and old.

Blanche was reticent no more,
confident in that good arm of hers.
Her smile brightened with life and glee,
"Come on, youngster, come wrestle me,
I'm just eighty-three year old little Blanche
and you with your youth have both arms strong.
Come on, youngster, let the wrestling begin now."

Blanche placed her good elbow on the table
and awaited the youngster's paused response.
The youth had a hunch she might not win,
and in front of a lot of folks intently watching.

Elbows on the table, the contest got started
between these young and old sturdy arms.
And struggle they did, their arms well matched,
and they swayed on the table to and fro.
"I'll beat you," Blanche said, her bold voice awakened
with a strength no one had ever guessed she possessed.

Well, Blanche did win the match that day
with her muscular arm strong and aged,
and her only arm that still worked.
Blanche was transformed completely in the match
as folks cheered her mighty arm on,
and she laughed in glee as her strong arm won.

There was an important lesson I learned that day,
I who was the twenty-five year old youngster.
Youth takes strength for granted in life,
yet this youth lost the match to age,
to a strength that was practiced every day.

I learned that day to never underestimate old age,
nor assume I know what kind of strength exists.
I picture Blanche, shyly painting with hesitance,
and that mighty strong spirit that prevailed.
Blanche was a fierce fighter as well as a bold painter.

November 2002

Hatred

Hatred is a festering wound
of anger, hurt, pride, and judgment.
Hatred is a wound that is unhealed,
festering unseen and unattended,
spewing poison that wounds spirits
deep, damaging, within and without.
It is very difficult to under tand hatred.
It seems such a waste of life energy.
Hatred is big anger unheard and then stored
until it explodes its poison built up over time.

Anger protects us when we are willing to hear it.
Anger speaks of intrusion, insensitivity, and pain.
Anger tells us that something is bothering us,
about something important that needs healing.

Hatred is weapons grade anger in stealth,
a plastic explosive that awaits a trigger.
Hatred has toppled many tall buildings,
great empires and vast civilizations.
Hatred poisons and wastes human caring.
Hatred kills with excuses for its cause.

Yes, hatred is very difficult to understand.
Perhaps not understanding is God's grace.
There is a choice of action with any anger.
Anger can seek to create or destroy.
God is able to heal raw anger and hurt
and that healing can then create new life.

To choose to heal the raw anger we feel
creates much hope and possibility,
opportunity for the joy and life we seek
in the inner parts of our soul.
Hatred however ugly can be healed,
one anger at a time in God's own time.
Hatred is not a match for God's grace.

July 2001

Leslie Anne Miller

Sexuality

Cheap sex gushes from my television set,
the sexuality of the young, thin, and beautiful
and only the very young, thin, and beautiful.
Watching it leaves me disgusted and discouraged.

There, sexuality is just an exercise of intercourse,
not an act of love.
There it is about separation not union,
about attraction not truth,
about appearance not spirit.

In the spirit, sexuality is part of one's being,
part of who one is with a soul mate through the day.
Together, it is the making of their bed in the morning,
sharing salads and meals, taking the dogs out,
sharing thoughts, watching a sunset, gazing at stars.
It is sharing laughter and sharing sorrow.
It is souls joining in the heights and in the depths.

Commercial sexuality presents muddy puddles.
Loving sexuality is as vast as the deep sea.

Mature sexuality is joining souls not bodies.
Careless sexuality is joining bodies not souls.
Maturity needs time and good role models
who demonstrate what love is and can be,
who teach sexuality as an act of mature love,
who turn off the television and the gush of cheap sex,
and take the time each day to demonstrate love.

March 1999

Roy

Roy's joy was activities, posted daily for all to see.
Sadly, Roy no longer had a sense of time,
so he was most often waiting many hours,
blocking the hallway with his wheelchair,
asking every person passing by
when the special activity began.
Roy needed help to sit up in his chair,
more often than not he was sliding out,
and he drooled when he spoke with a spitting wet voice.
Truth be known he had quite an odor, as well,
and was often in dire need of intimate care.
He resisted this care because of his fear
that he might miss out on the grand activity.
He often pestered, asking everyone the time,
while he slid prone in his chair
with sputtering spit with his speech,
having an odor that made folks steer clear.

Yet, there was a special magical quality Roy had,
despite the intimate care he always resisted.
It was his eyes so excited and lit up in wonder,
like a small child awaiting Santa Claus's lap.
It was impossible to ignore his childlike eyes,
even while he sputtered, pestered, and slid.
His excitement was contagious, you see,
for anyone who encountered dear Roy.
His excitement transformed the hallway,
where elders waited like a crowd of young,
and all despite Roy being a crowd of one.

One day, there was an ice cream social,
and Roy had dozens of questions.
His eyes were lit up in glitter that day.
He glowed bright sitting in the hallway.
But ice cream for Roy was not meant to be,
because this sputtering marvelous dear man,
died twenty minutes before ice cream began.

In thinking about living and dying,
then and for these many years since,
perhaps the lesson and wonder of Roy,
was that dying in excited anticipation of life
was to die very well after all.

November 2001

An Important Thought

I can be critical of people, and I can be critical of myself.
This habit does not honor me.
This habit does not honor people.

I am replacing this criticism with forgiveness.
I can forgive people and I can forgive myself.
This habit soothes and honors me.
This habit soothes and honors people.

When I love people, I'm better at loving myself.
When I speak love to people, I speak love to myself.
When I am offering love to people,
I am receiving love offered to me.
These habits replenish and nourish me.
These habits replenish and nourish people.

The things I say to myself are as important
as the things I say to other people.
The things that I say to people in my mind
are as important as the things I say in person.
Thoughts are just as important as actions.

The things I give myself, I give to other people.
The things I give to people, I give to myself.
What I cultivate in myself, I can cultivate in people.
What I cultivate in people, I cultivate in myself.
The garden I tend within
can be seen in the garden I tend without.
It's an important thought.

July 2001

Leslie Anne Miller

Suffering Purpose

There are some folks who have a difficult purpose,
a suffering purpose to find the purpose of suffering.
One purpose might be relief of suffering for others,
a purpose birthed from the suffering needing relief.

Birth emerges out of the labor of suffering.
Within that suffering is purpose and potential,
love and growth and meaning.
Birth emerging takes time.

The world is in need of meaning for suffering.

Suffering is most often avoided, ignored,
pushed away by the stressed and self-involved
with no time or compassion for suffering.
Most push into it, around it, over it, and flee.
Suffering is very difficult to notice.
Noticing suffering takes courage and time.
Noticing suffering is desperately needed
in a world where so many people suffer,
many needlessly, in pain and alone.

Suffering can inspire efforts to find relief from suffering,
a purpose desperately needed for those who suffer.
Suffering can inspire compassion, courage and introspection,
intimacy, understanding and a pause.
Suffering clings desperately to God for meaning.
Meaning in suffering takes thought and grace.
Suffering has a suffering purpose for God.
Our task is to seek that purpose.

November 2002

Chocolate

Chunks and chips and sprinkles,
syrups and creams and truffles,
light and dark and milky.

Chocolate celebrates joy,
chocolate consoles despair.

Chocolate can nurture every day.
Chocolate can delight an occasion.

Chocolate wins hearts and minds.
Chocolate wins fans and praise.

Chocolate convinces the doubtful.
Chocolate has no doubt for the convinced.
Chocolate is passion pursued.
Chocolate endures in memory.

Chocolate is a beloved favorite.
Chocolate is beloved by children, young and old.

I need some chocolate right here and right now.
Chocolate tempts the writer and reader
of poetry about chocolate.

November 2002

Leslie Anne Miller

Wisdom

Today is a sunny lazy type of day.
I awoke feeling quiet and thoughtful.
This quiet led me to a tranquility within.

There, I experienced a connection with myself
that I was unaware of
during the busy times of my life.

The beginning of wisdom evolves from quiet.
Wisdom returns to the quiet.
Reflection is a path to wisdom,
a journey within to find connection
with ourselves and with our God.

Today, I give wisdom some time in reflection
that evolves from a quiet solitude
and leads me to a place of connection.

Taking time for quiet solitude and reflection,
prayer and guidance is a path to wisdom
which is a cherished gift from God.

December 1996

Summer

The dust blows hot across the straw grass
and scraggy bushes.
When the sun beats against my brow, I feel scorched.
I feel charred.
The merciless August heat has finally ignited into flames.
I miss the gentle spring and long for the brisk coolness of fall.

I remember the summer of my life,
it pushed me into life with vast energy and zest.
And I remember the pressured race for power.
Power that can ignite,
scorching people into charred cinders,
casting flames in the heat to burn the innocent.

Disability ended the summer of my life.
For me the race is over for power and might.
And, I no longer care about relentless pursuit.

Though the heat of summer is about me,
searching, I found a shady place.
Here I find refreshment and moments to reflect,
time to let God take root in my soul.
Here there is gentle respite and peace.

I reflect upon summer, and listen to the lessons it brings.
I let God create a serene oasis about me and within.
And leave power and might to those willing to burn.

December 1997

Leslie Anne Miller

Gladys

She swept by me in her flowing caftan gown,
as she motored smoothly down the hallway,
her mangled fingers atop the hand controls
her mangled feet discreetly covered by her gown.

She was bigger than life when she entered a room,
and her social skills were superb.
No disagreement, however loud,
was a match for her crooning voice,
that spoke with a soft southern lilt,
that quieted frayed nerves and minds.

In time, her glowing presence transformed
a gaggle of disparate folks,
from a mess of desperate separateness
into a charmingly and warm social whole.

From Gladys, I learned that beauty
emanates not from a body without flaws
but rather from a quiet grace within
and an ability to let that grace glow.

November 2002

Belonging

In the world of disability,
belonging means having access.
When faced with barriers,
it is easy to feel unwelcomed,
unwanted, rejected,
isolated, and withdrawn.

Belonging really begins
with reaching and risking.
Barriers are more often due
to ignorance than intention.
Faced with disability,
sometimes it is much easier
for others to do nothing
than to risk not knowing
what to say or to do.

Belonging begins with courage
and the grace of God.
Belonging begins with experiment
and a commitment to try.
Belonging begins with beginning,
one small step at a time.
Belonging begins with courage
and a belief in God.
God's grace has no barriers for disability,
the door is open
for all those who seek and ask.

October 2001

Floating

Illness interrupted the direction of my life.
I felt angry at my loss and inadequacy.
I tried often to return to my former self.

I insisted on swimming upstream.

It was a time of despair and failure.
I persisted with things I could no longer do.
People became angry at their inability to help.
My despair became theirs and
we suffered our connection.

Unbearable suffering left me weary.
Endless weary left me searching.
Searching left me changed.

I now focus on the things I am still able to do.
I learn the lessons of my life as they are today.
I have grown a new inner self.
I have learned to float and follow the stream.

People express joy at their ability to help.
My learning and success become theirs and
we celebrate our connection.

I am learning the ability to float through life.
Life teaches every day with new challenges.
Illness has caused me to search,
and searching left me changed,
floating with the stream,
enjoying life along the way,
doing what I can
to continue to grow
a new self,
floating.

March 1999

I Do Matter

I feel as though I live outside the mainstream.

People rush by me going elsewhere.
Cars speed by me going somewhere.
I hobble along going here and there,
moving in the slow lane of our culture.

Yet, here on the fringes of the mainstream,
I breathe.
I pray.
I think.
I decide.

Life continues on with all the time there is,
going here and there in the slow lane of life.
My little neighborhood,
well traveled, is somewhere.

I am someone who is actually quite alive.
Life matters not in how meager or extensive,
or how ordinary or how gifted we are.
Life only matters in how it is lived.
Life only matters lived with love.

I matter,
living hobbled,
living slow,
living loving,
and living well.

October 2001

Leslie Anne Miller

Shadows

Losses shadow my life, haunting me
with memories of past days in the sun.

It helps immensely to remember
that the sun shines beyond shadow.
The sun shines beyond wind and squalls,
trees and flowers,
puppies and kittens,
babies and people large and small.
The sun shines beyond moments.
The sun is a reminder of the eternal,
the eternal that exists beyond loss and shadow.

Shadows are a darkened reminder
that the sun still shines beyond.
Shadows have motion and change.
Shadows reach out for the sun.
Shadows come and go and
shadows ebb and tide.

And so it is with loss,
losses that shadow life.
Shadows are a reminder of lost gifts,
gifts that have motion and change.
Gifts reach out for sun and possibility.
Losses are a definition
that comes and goes or stays.
Losses must accept the dark shadows,
because shadows can dance with the sun.
The sun always reflects the eternal
that exists beyond loss and shadow.

October 2001

Growth

Growth is exciting for a child.
Growth is challenging for a student.
Growth is rewarding for an adult.

Failing capabilities can interrupt growth,
the growth of past conception,
trying to climb for a summit,
with failing capability,
grasping at branches
when sliding into an abyss
is a different type of growth.
The summit is perhaps a memory.
The abyss is perhaps a certain possibility.

With failing capability, to grasp a branch,
to dig in hard with heels,
to slow the slide is growth.
To enjoy the view,
while sliding into the abyss,
rather than fearing the demise,
is a different type of growth.

It is worthy and noble growth.
It is courageous growth.

To enjoy the view
despite the slide
is a cultivated growth.
It is thoughtful growth
ands emotional growth.
It is spiritual growth.

Leslie Anne Miller

Growth with failing capability
is about being very grateful
for hands to grasp the branches
and for heels to slow the slide,
for moments to enjoy the view.
Growth is in the gratitude we possess.
Gratitude with failing capabilities
is a summit unto its own,
a summit that is a difficult
yet cherished type of growth.
It is growth that reaches for God.

October 2001

Uniquely Being

Life is unique to each person.
Each person has a different response,
different support,
a different purpose,
a different journey.
Each human being is unique.

The challenge is uniquely being a human being.
Uniquely being is reaching deep inside
and listening to our inner self.
Only there do we find our spirit
and the direction,
support and journey
to honor our soul.

Uniquely being a unique being is a daunting task.
Being a unique human being is a gift of birth.
Uniquely being is a gift of grace.

Grace acknowledged is a spiritual journey.
Grace cultivated is uniquely being.

Gratitude cultivates grace
and grace cultivates gratitude.
Those who have gratitude for grace
are the human beings
in touch with uniquely being.

October 2001

Leslie Anne Miller

Potatoes

Such a lowly birth beneath the earth
in the womb of dirt, worms and ants,
dug out, sorted, washed and cleaned
and tossed into a rough dark sack,
along with other lucky spuds
to have birthed beneath the earth.

Shipped off to markets, groceries in malls
and placed in a great vegetable land,
hauled off in cars, tossed into lairs
that are dark, very cool, and dry.
Then, one by one, yanked out of a sack
to be washed and cleaned yet again,
then off to the knife, the slice, the chop,
the boil, the bake, the fry.

When then at last placed on a plate
and admired by the forks and spoons,
placed by the fish or meat or fowl,
adorned by vegetables festive bright
of green, red, purple, and orange,
it's a royal display from a lowly birth
of a potato born beneath the earth,
to be admired, chewed, and chomped,
in order to nourish, sustain, and grow
future planters of new potatoes.

July 1999

Meaning

What is it that gives life meaning?
Is it doing things or having things?
Making things or thinking things?
Is it work or consumerism?
Perhaps family or country?
Is it action or thought or, prayer?

Art gives life meaning.
Art is a form of prayer.
Clay, canvas, brush, and paint,
draw me to imagine and create.
I am hungry, yearning, searching, nourished,
refreshed and renewed, surprised and delighted
learning of God in art.

Gratitude gives life meaning
and gratitude is a form of prayer.
Gratitude comes from grace.
Grace is noticing life.
God is in flowers, creatures large and small,
people of all colors and cultures.

Prayer gives life meaning.
Prayer opens my spirit to God's love,
to me, and through me to others.

People gives life meaning.
Celebrating people is a form of prayer.
I give who I am and I receive who they are.
I am blessed by God in relationships.

Love gives life meaning.
Love is a form of prayer.
Love is what I was born to be.
Love is giving all that I am.
Love is the meaning of life.
Love is from God and God is love.

November 2001

Leslie Anne Miller

Fully Alive

To be fully alive and savor the moment
that moment by moment is life,
seems lost in the stress of the lists and tasks
of a culture that is rushing somewhere by.

The push and shove, the right here, right now,
the mine, no time, no way,
the tasks, the projects, the proposals on time,
no room, no space, no time.

The house, the car, the clothes on credit
and groceries on occasion too,
deadlines and debts, responsibilities that mount,
piled high is the debt mountain that we own.

But no, you say, no way, no how,
no time to think or choose.
It's how everyone lives today, don't you know,
in this culture, the most advanced in the world.

Those people on the side, watching people whiz by,
might have something to say
about the fast lives racing by.
Isn't it true we have all the time there is?
Truth is, most have little time to live life.

To not savor the moment, which is all we have
is to really not have lived life fully alive.

October 2001

We are One

In a busy world,
we believe we are separate.
We live in separate houses
and drive separate cars.
We visit separate places
and pursue separate interests.
We have separate intentions
and we live separate lives.

Yet, we breathe the same air and we affect the air quality.
We eat our food and we affect food distribution.
We go to work and we affect work quality.
We live our lives and we affect other lives.

Every living human, creature or plant,
needs to belong to each other.
Each interacts with each other and affects each other.
Each of us is unique.
Each of us is a part of the whole.

We are one.
Something we might consider.
Something we need to remember.

We are one.
It matters not ignorance. It matters not knowledge.
It matters how we act. Separate or together.
Creating or destroying. Alive or dying.
Survival or extinction.

We are one. It matters.
Today, now, in this moment,
and each moment in time.

October 2001

Leslie Anne Miller

The Puzzle

Losses have broken my goals and dreams,
leaving them scattered about me
in disparate puzzle pieces.
My emotions are scattered as well,
there is confusion, anger, then resolve.

New puzzle pieces come together slowly
until the larger picture begins to emerge.
I only need to cope with one piece at a time.
I only need to believe in a larger picture,
perhaps something different than my dreams.

I only need to begin to create it,
one moment, one piece at a time,
and if a piece doesn't fit into the whole,
perhaps there is another that fits better.

Today I create my dream, one moment at a time,
by picking up one puzzle piece at a time
of the small fragments that now are my life.
Each piece, some newly created
and some that are jagged and worn,
are the pieces of a newly created goal,
the pieces of a new imagined dream,
and the pieces of a new possibility
for my life.
Then there will be a new puzzle.

November 2002

Potential

Potential is a possible consideration.
We can ask what is the problem,
which does needs to be asked.
And then afterwards, perhaps,
we can ask what is the potential?

Loss has difficult moments and challenges,
more difficult to manage when badly wounded.
Perhaps more an elusive but intriguing thought
is the potential.

Problems unresolved create sorrow in the heart.
Problems unsolved can be life's heavy laden.

Potential is about creating possibilities.
Potential can lift up the spirit.
Potential can regenerate the heart.

Losses cannot be ignored or wounds deepen.
Problems cannot be swept away or they haunt.
Losses can be paralyzing,
yet it's helpful to know,
losses leave possibilities
and possibilities have potential.

A person is not their loss.
A loss is multifaceted,
yet amidst it is possibility for potential.
When losses teach about finding the courage
to explore, then possibilities for potential arise.

Losses have potential because potential cannot be extinguished.

Only ignored.

October 2001

Leslie Anne Miller

Frank

He sat, arms folded, waiting for dining to open,
with his false teeth peeking out his shirt pocket.
If asked why it was so that he took his teeth out to go
to dinner where he might use his teeth.

Well, it's simple he'd explain, it's really quite plain,
teeth that get used get dirty.
So, to protect them from grime,
he daily took the time
to remove them into his breast shirt pocket.

Frank was the only one to point out this logic
and who carried his teeth this way.
That's why he's dear in my memory
for his lesson on preserving clean teeth.

One other thing made Frank quite special.
It was the fact that, though he could not see,
he loved to sing whenever he felt the urge,
which could be anytime or anywhere at all.

One day, we took Frank out to the symphony,
teeth in for the occasion too.
It was during the long intermission
when Frank felt the inspiration to sing.

He bellowed out "Swing Low, Sweet Chariot,"
which happened to be his favorite song,
to the amusement of hundreds of people
finding their way back for the symphony to begin.

Frank had two special things quite unique,
clean teeth in his shirt pocket during meals,
and the love of singing anytime, anywhere
that he felt the inspiration to sing.

October 2000

Passion

The attorney's eyes took in the witness
with an intensity that was palpable to see,
his passion for justice was etched on his face.
His knowledge and skill about the law
are the tools of his passion.

Passion is the force behind justice and law.

The eyes of the artist reflect intensity quite visible,
his passion for creativity is etched on his face.
His colors and shapes are the tools of his passion.

Passion is the force behind creative expression.

The eyes of the soldier exploded with an intensity
that was deafening,
His passion for this fight was etched on his face.
His weapons and bravery are the tools of his passion.

Passion is the force behind justice in war.

The eyes of the person with loss filled with tears of grief.
The passion for remembrance is etched on his face.
Courage and strength are the tools of new life.

Passion is the force behind strength for remembrance.

Passion is the force behind life,
living with passion,
living fully,
fully alive.

July 2000

Leslie Anne Miller

Intelligence

Intelligence with ability is multifaceted.
It is not enough to accumulate knowledge.
Knowledge that is not utilized
to create productive contribution,
or to optimize living,
is a booby prize.

Intelligence with spirituality is multifaceted.
It is not enough to investigate possibility.
Investigation without commitment
is a choice not to commit.
Commitment is essential to spirituality.

Intelligence with relationships is multifaceted.
It is not enough to learn about relationships.
Relationships are about risk, the risk of rejection.
Knowledge of emotion without relationship is deadening.

Intelligence with wisdom is multifaceted.
It is not enough just to know.
Knowing without acting is a waste of grace.
Knowing without the grace of compassion
is intelligence that is hardening.

Intelligence with gratitude is multifaceted.
It is not enough to accept gratitude.
Gratitude is about accepting grace.
Gratitude is about sharing.
Knowing without gratitude is arrogance.
Knowing without sharing is selfish.

Intelligence is a gift of grace from God,
a grace that needs to be shared
with the world.

December 2001

Laughter

Cancer was destroying Ed's body.

As his body became withered and weak,
his spirit grew vibrant and strong.

A friend sent him a joke to cheer him,
a quarter made from small change
glued to a large industrial washer.

A twinkle began to appear in Ed's eyes
when a visitor inquired about the strange object,
sitting on his hospital bedside table.

Again and again, he loved to joke
about the unusual quarter he possessed,
his enthusiasm and joy were contagious
to everyone he encountered in his room.

After a short time, Ed did die,
bequeathing a treasure of courage,
vulnerability and laughter with poignancy.

Laughter is a moment of good health.
Laughter when shared with suffering
is spiritual connection.
Laughter in suffering is spiritual inspiration.

God is a God of laughter
in the face of suffering and death.

It's a mystery of God;
laughter amidst suffering.

November 2001

Leslie Anne Miller

A Helping Hand

My taxes support government programs
that help people who are struggling in life.
There are programs for those impoverished,
unemployed or elderly,
or struggling with disability.

But programs do not replace the caring
of family, friends, and neighbors.
Caring is reaching out a helping hand.

But, I pay taxes to fund programs that help people.
That is enough! I did my part!

No, it is not enough.
Taxes are not life-giving.
Touch is life-giving.
Empathy is life-giving.
Compassion is life-giving.

A helping hand is personal.
A helping hand is grace given.
A helping hand is a gift shared.

Government is not personal.
Government has no compassionate touch.
Government has no grace.

What is personal is a helping hand that cares.
To those God has gifted, he expects much.
He expects a helping hand to those in need.

November 2001

Critters

I am grateful for my critters,
their souls attached to mine,
their eyes aglow with love,
their bodies warm with mine.

I feel sad there are critters,
with souls wanting to give,
with eyes aglow with love,
and lives that abruptly end.

I wish that all the critters,
their souls attached to ours,
with eyes aglow with love,
could speak of wanted lives.

Oh that all of God's critters,
their souls attached to ours,
with eyes aglow with love,
could get the love they deserved.

We'd be a better people,
our souls attached to theirs,
with eyes aglow with love,
critters beloved by God,
in a world of critter love.

February 2003

Ode to the End of Stigma

Stigma is a stereotype, deficiency or flaw.
Stigma is a blemish, a raw or angry bruise.
Stigma is a shame that people seek to hide.
Stigma is feeling like a heavy lead burden.
Stigma is feeling less, guilty for being alive.
Stigma is a judgment of rejected human being.

Stigma is deep wounding. It emanates out of fear.
It separates and isolates. It makes one small and sad.
We consider people less. We judge with harsh labels.
We call someone a cripple, a moron or a lunatic,
an object for rejection and scorn.

Stigma happens in a relationship.
One is much better, more capable or strong,
more handsome or wealthy, educated or refined.
Thank God for the power of choice we possess
to choose to not participate in belittling labels.
Joining stigma is not who we want to be.

Being stigmatized does indeed happen to me.
People can be frightened of declining health.
They believe their health is something deserved
until their health fails and they are stigmatized.
It might happen in their declining health
by people frightened of their own decline.
Stigma does not deserve our cooperation.

I choose today to be all that I can be
because I am not my body, rather a spirit.
My spirit continues to grow wings
as my health and strength decline,
until one day my spirit will fly high
long after my body finally died.
Here is to the end of the stigmas
that diminish our great land so capable of hope
for everyone's dreams and plans.

Here's to the beginning of offering hope
to anyone despite their problems.
Here's to the beginning of sharing love
with every spirit we meet and greet.
Sharing is a long tradition of our great land,
so capable of hope for everyone's dreams and plans.

February 2000

Leslie Anne Miller

Beliefs

Who we believe we are is an idea in our minds.
What we believe is important
in life and love and purpose.
Who we believe we are is who we have become.
It affects how we make all the decisions in our lives.

It's important to look at our childhood beliefs
that don't work as adults or give us relief.
Beliefs about sadness, gladness or grace
need sifting to keep only those that work.
We need to be aware that some of our beliefs
are buried deep within in our minds
and will take our commitment to change.

Maturing what we believe is a lifelong task.
Some folks live old beliefs in utter despair.
They blame life and people for all their problems.
Their life is about crisis, distress, and cynicism.
They don't realize there are other beliefs
and other paths to discover
that could offer healing and peace.

Liking what we believe is a good thing to cultivate,
it's possible to believe in stability and hope.
Folks that work to tend the garden of their beliefs,
are those that can bring the flowers to our world.
They believe they can create healing, hope, and love.
Choosing beliefs becomes grace and gratitude as well.
Changing beliefs is contagious
when people see the healing it brings.

Happiness has nothing to do with life's struggles.
We can come to realize that happiness is found
almost anywhere we choose to have gratitude.
When we're grateful people and live gratitude,
we find a precious gift for our spirit
and one we can share with the world.

March 2003

Stan

"The old projector isn't working again.
Could you please come and help us, Stan?"
"Ah, well, OK," he would grumble softly
as he slowly throttled down the hall.
"Do you think it's going to work, Stan?"
"Ah, well let me see," he said quietly
as he peered into the aged machine.
When Stan said nothing, we all worried
that there'd be no film that night
or worse, only half of a John Wayne film.

"Oh, wonderful, Stan, thank you much,
you got it working yet again!!"
"Ah, yes," he said, as everyone clapped
and returned their gaze to the screen.

Stan spoke quite rarely, often not at all.
Often he lumbered about the hallway,
lingering a moment to watch people
and then slowly sauntering away.
Mostly, he fixed the aged projector
on film night for an audience of the old.
They awaited the evening entertainment
after a trying and vexing, long day
surviving their health's slow demise.

"Oh Stan, please come help us again!
The projector won't work anymore!
We were all looking forward to this film,
it's John Wayne, don't you know.
It's getting late and bedtime looms!
Who sleeps on half of John Wayne?"

"Ah, OK," he would say, closing his book
and putting it on his nightstand.
I'll be there soon, he would mumble softly
as he sauntered down the long hallway
to rescue our projector once again.
"Oh, look everyone! Stan has come
to look at our old projector again!
This man, our Stan, he's the real John Wayne!
He once again came to our rescue!"
Stan, as always, slowly lumbered away.

January 2003

A Small Voice

A small voice cries. Where it comes from is not clear.
It sounds fragile and vulnerable, afraid and unsure.
I feel like hiding from the tears welling up
slowly out the depths of my soul.
When I am afraid, I tend to I hide,
wrapping myself in a cloak of capability.
I stay busy attending to important affairs
and muffle the small sound of the tears.
Still the tears well up and the tiny voice grows louder.
I do not have time to listen and I do not want to pause.
I have these important things to accomplish.
Yet, I sense a need to honor the tears within.

Pain is a valuable teacher when I do listen.
Sometimes it is a small voice within me.
If I don't listen, the voice grows louder,
crying out for compassion
and patience amidst the turmoil inside.
The voice within struggles to be heard
and hopes to be understood, if I give it time
away from my pressing affairs.
If I continue to suppress it, I'll be mostly numb.
Living life numb creates a life that is dulled.
No longer do I know what's important,
nor can I tell anyone what I do feel,
and I can't decide if I care.

Listening to the voice empowers it to teach
important lessons for my journey in life.
Listening to pain and learning its lessons
leaves me better able to listen
to the pain and turmoil of others.
It becomes a gift I have to give
and for that ability, I am grateful.
Listening breaks the habit of hiding
and creates a life that is important.
Feelings let me know that I care
and that I can be a gift to the world.

Leslie Anne Miller

The important thing in my life now
is the integrity of the expression
of God within who guides me.
God speaks clearly if I will listen
to that a small soft voice inside.

March 2000

The Ferry Ride

Despite the disability permit displayed on my car,
the ferry employee was livid
about being inconvenienced by my request.
"If you aren't well, why don't you stay home?"
You're not some privileged person."
Her annoyance and anger permeated the air.
Finally, with reluctance,
she assisted my boarding.

Disability involves continuous challenge.
There are ongoing obstacles to overcome.
Barrier-filled streets and buildings,
pugnacious policy and people,
are just some of the difficulties encountered
venturing into the world with a disability.

The struggle with obstacles is worth the difficulties.
It was a beautiful day for a ferry ride.
Sun glistened on the waves, warming my spirits.
Seagulls soared above the water.
Wind scattered the clouds through the sky.
Memory of the lack of compassion faded.
I was glad for the challenge of the ferry ride.
It was a wonderful day to be alive,
a precious memory to savor.

It is worth the struggle to be fully alive.

April 2000

Adrian

Silently, Adrian watched, his eyes intent on knowing,
in a language of glances quiet and subtle.
It was an encounter of eye connection
that spoke of friendship and presence.

His Eskimo culture was learned in a remote village
where communicating was with eyes and movement.
Adrian would glance left or right and up or down,
each movement saying something of note,
that was well understood by his Eskimo friend
who communicated his understanding in silence.

His old Eskimo friend could not speak at all
but used his eyes well to say what he meant.
Adrian often wheeled his chair to his friend's bed
near the window where mountains greeted him.

For hours he would stay, his chair touching the bed,
communicating his friendship and care.
The power of silence and presence was there,
a quiet bond between Adrian and his friend.

More than anyone I ever have known,
Adrian taught me most
about the power of silence and presence,
not talking but listening to the power of a bond,
that went where language could not reach.

My relationships are changed having known Adrian
because silence and presence expand connection
beyond words that are inadequate to express
the power and bond and promise
that exists between family and friends.

March 2003

Ode to E-Mail

It used to be letters full of junk mail, bills, and greetings.
Today we have e-mail with its instant greetings
as well as attachments, pictures, junk mail, and spam.
In addition to junk mail arriving by post, we now have it arriving instantly,
not to mention bringing instant viruses that can shut the computer down.

E-mail is instant communication, demanding instant response,
developing instant relationships, divulging instant threats,
or discussing instant intimacy.

It seems that e-mail has created an instant speed of life,
instant want of response, leaving us spoiled and distressed,
burdened, irritated and often very tired.

Has e-mail made our lives better or created new demands
that stretch our lives thin with no time to search within?

Has e-mail created a cost that each of us has to pay,
a toll, a new drain of time, on top of stress in the commute
and the longer days at work?

So, what is there really to do?
Can instant communication help?
It quickens notes from friends or family but frequent advertisements as well.
Perhaps it allows for a quicker response to a question or upset as well.
A group of people can quickly receive a joke or thought about life
and without the cost of postage either.

I guess e-mail can help or hinder us depending on how we use it.
For myself, I check e-mail less often, three times a week.
I have balance in my life between its convenience and costs.
Like most things, it really depends on our decisions
about how its purpose can fit in our lives.
It's a good thought on progress, I suppose,
to remember the need for balance
and responsibility for our decisions as well.

Leslie Anne Miller

E-mail isn't leaving, of that I'm quite convinced.
One day we may need periodic vacations
to remember life without instant e-mail!

February 2003

Parents

I am grateful to my parents for a precious gift,
the gift of having been born.
Deep within my mind I hear their voices.
I learned how to treat myself and other people
from how they treated me.

Responsibility for my life is totally mine.
I have memories and beliefs,
habits and dreams that are similar to my parents.
I have many that are also quite different.
I am the person I have become.

I'm committed to honoring individuality
and also treasuring my wonderful parents.
I am a part of a family,
and I am separate, uniquely me.
With their guidance and foundation,
I forge my own path in life
to claim my destiny, however big or small.

I'm grateful to my parents for giving me life
and also for a unique life experience.

I'm very grateful for who I've become.
with the launch into life they provided me.

April 2000

Leslie Anne Miller

Dark Nights

Things have fallen apart again.
Capabilities I had regained are lost.
My hopes crash in splinters about me.
My spirit is in a dark night and despair overwhelms me.
I have experienced this dark night before.
It is a always a difficult time and challenges my spirit.
Losses occur. Losses are grieved. Recovery is slow.

I have learned to wait on the dawn of a new sunrise.
Eventually, I know that it will come,
quiet and slow, adorned in the majesty of hope.
Its arrival is a moment of true grace.
Its arrival is a moment of gratitude for life.

The burden of despair is dark and heavy.
If it were not for hope, it is too much to bear.
The night might diminish the spirit
but for the hope of another dawn.
Despite any anguish, I always cling to hope.
I pray to transcend the dark moments.
I reach out to someone who I can trust.

The dawn is more poignant
because of the dark night of struggle.
I need only take notice of its arrival
and appreciate the radiant hues it brings.
When a dark night happens in my life,
I need to remember that always
there is the hope for a new dawn
either here or perhaps beyond.

August 2000

Music

This morning I turned on my clock radio.
The music was a quartet of melodic flute and violin.
My stress melted into a quiet peace as
the music danced in my thoughts.
The music comforted my spirit.

Music is a lyrical tapestry
woven with
threads of sound and pause.
I was woven into the music,
part of its story
and its story a part of me.

Soon the music swept me further aloft
and my spirit began to soar
higher and higher to touch the sky
and frolic amongst the clouds.

Music inspires my journey.
Music creates song in my soul.
Music takes my spirit aloft
and touches heaven's gate.

Thank God for music. And, I do.

January 1995

Leslie Anne Miller

Kitty

Gaunt and wizened, she hovered by the door
to pounce on anyone entering our home of aged folks.
Before they had walked six feet from the door,
she would pounce on the uninformed prey.
Gaunt and wizened, she would beg them to stop
and give her just a small crust of bread,
as they were starving her to death in this home.
Wheeling along as they walked,
grabbing for a hand to hold,
she'd beg them to please stop a moment,
as she wanted only a small crust of bread,
she'd had nothing to eat for days.
Could they stop but a moment to listen?
Could they spare a small crust of bread?

If the visitor stopped, Kitty would display
the bruises on both of her arms evidence of mistreatment.
Oh please, she would plead, again and again,
would they give just a small crust of bread,
to a tortured and starving soul?
Very soon, a staff person would arrive
to extricate the bewildered prisoner
from the gaunt starving begging soul.
She would explain to Kitty that she was well fed,
and her bruises were from her screeching fights,
when it took four aides to give her a bath.
She was bruised by her thrashing arms
in the soggy fight that would ensue.

Then turning to the visitor, the staff remarked that
Kitty was 100 years old, the home's oldest resident.
It was a fact that brought the home much pride,
and a fact that brought Kitty pride as well.
Kitty would smile her gaunt wizen grin
and then snare the visitor's hand.

Proudly, she'd sit straight in her chair
to say that she had been around for a while
and that she knew a thing or two.
Then she'd release her snared hand
and the visitor could finally escape,
ushered away quickly by the staff.
Kitty would sit alone for a moment or two
then wheel back down to the entrance,
to await her next visiting prey.

Despite Kitty's profound confusion
entrapping prey at the entrance door,
begging for a small crust of bread,
and professing starvation and mistreatment,
the home was very proud to have Kitty,
the home's unique and colorful eldest,
because just as she was, she was special,
a feisty, determined, and persistent fighter
who had lived a very long life
and knew a thing or two.

July 2000

Leslie Anne Miller

Endurance

Runners train to complete long marathons.
Climbers train to climb lofty mountains.
Skiers train for competitive Grand Slaloms.
An athlete's training requires great challenge
coupled with fierce determination
and perseverance to succeed.

Athletes provide unique inspiration
for the endurance that disability demands.
Disability is lifelong marathons
climbing uphill to increased capability
or maintaining strength to slow the slide.

Disability sometimes crushes life dreams.
It takes creativity to find new aspirations and
an open spirit with belief that
there is life and possibility to explore,
as long as a person is yet alive.

The story of a life journey continues to the end.
The end of life is the finish line for
the grand marathon of life disability.
Until then, the challenge is living well, glad for a life to live.
The endurance marathon is living a good life, fully alive.

June 2000

Franky

Frank had been an aerospace engineer
before an accident claimed his abilities.
His head, arms, and legs were frozen in pretzel,
and he twisted and jerked without warning.
His speech was difficult to understand,
so he rarely tried to speak.
Each day, he was wheeled to the wet room,
for those who needed to be changed.
Placed in a row around the walls of the room,
was where many folks spent their day.

Meals were served in the wet room,
where nurse's aides fed their group,
filling several mouths at one time,
while encouraging their group to eat.
"Franky, eat your peas, they are good for you.
Come on, here's the fork, open your mouth,
these peas are really tasty to eat."
I sat in my office, listening to the aide.
I knew his mouth was already chocked with peas
and I anticipated his unique response.

"Foook yooo," he would explode, spraying peas
everywhere on faces, arms, and clothes.
"Fooook yooo," he would scream, spraying peas,
unloading his mouth of pea bullets.
"Foooook yooo," he would screech, spraying yet more
as he emptied the last load in his mouth.

YES!! I would think, Frank has claimed again,
the dignity of an adult human being.
Call Frank, Franky, and stuff his mouth,
and his anger would build a mouth canon,
"Foook Yoo," he would howl as he splattered food
on faces and clothing and walls.

And at that moment, Frank made his point
and everyone understood his speech.
For that time at least, his dignity was restored,
and an aide had learned a life lesson.
Don't treat an adult like they are a child,
just because they are in need of your help,
just because they are disabled and helpless.
Dignity must be first, more important than peas,
and more important than soiled faces and walls.

January 2000

Rush Hour

I wanted to feel like I belonged at work
but fatigue made it an increasing challenge.
Stressed by ideals, compassion fatigued,
people had neither time nor energy
to include a person trying to keep up
in a work of rushing deadlines.
They could not take time to understand.
I could not do things their way.
I felt like I was not enough
and I realized that I didn't belong.

They rushed on past and not fitting in,
I had a scapegoat crash,
a hit and run of misunderstanding.
How dark that rush hour seemed,
lit by the flickering light of rushed ideals.
A scapegoat crash creates great pain,
wounds that are scars for a lifetime.
Those who scapegoat live in fear
of the vulnerability they sense.
Rush hour creates excuses for not caring.
Vulnerability might slow traffic.
They might themselves have a scapegoat crash.

I recovered from that hit and run of long ago
when my focus was those rushed deadlines.
I no longer participate in rush hour.
I have increasing disability
and have taken a quieter path,
where wheelchairs, walkers,
scooters, and canes
can travel safely in daylight
of the compassion and care
of those who are able to take the time
to notice and understand disability.

Leslie Anne Miller

I have found a path where I belong
and I am grateful to be alive
sharing time with folks like me
who travel the quiet path.
I enjoy having the time to share with companions
the beauty of the scenery we notice
and the blessings along this path.

June 2000

Scrambled Eggs

I ate my eggs soft boiled
a reflection of a life too soft,
a time when life was easier
and traffic seemed quieter too.

Today I eat scrambled eggs,
a reflection of a scrambled brain,
a time when life is much harder,
and traffic seems ever a mess.

Not that eggs are a reflection of life
or a reflection of traffic or a brain.
I'm only observing certain facts
that happen to be true about me.

I do eat scrambled eggs today,
and I preferred soft boiled then,
and life today does seem scrambled,
and life then did seem rather soft,
and traffic then indeed was quieter.
and traffic today is an incredible mess.

Not that scrambled eggs caused all these changes.
It's just that my life seems like scrambled eggs
and my brain and the traffic are scrambled too.

Perhaps life seems a bit scrambled to many folks,
perhaps driving scrambled freeways from work,
reflecting on the scramble of things yet to do
when they arrive home and then back to work.
Such a thought might scramble the heartiest of brains
who dare to ponder the scrambled eggs of life.

February 2003

Panic

My heart is pounding inside my chest.
My mind races from thought to thought.
Panic has begun to overwhelm me.
Perhaps, I won't get out of this crevasse.
I don't have the strength to climb and I'm frightened.

When panic wells up, I formulate a plan
for climbing when frightened and overwhelmed.
Panic just adds more bleakness to the crevasse.
I'll pause to rest and find the strength to climb.
I'll look for the light to see my way out.
I'll trust God with the challenge to survive.
I'll live this moment and hope for tomorrow.
This moment is enough of a life challenge.

I'll rest and calm my pounding heart.
I'll open my soul to God above
and receive grace to lift my spirit.
Grace can comfort and soothe fear.

I have climbed out of many a crevasse before,
looking up for the light of my spirit.
I'll find the will and strength to survive
and enjoy the challenge of my life,
because today, I still have my life.

With grace I climb the crevasse to the light,
never alone as my panic believes.
The grace of God is always at my side
giving me the confidence to try
no matter the depth of the dark crevasse.

January 1995

Beth

She sat silent, hands folded in her lap,
and always with her eyes cast down,
as if thinking of something important,
or contemplating something in depth.
She is seemingly oblivious to us all,
perhaps silent and not thinking at all.
To greet Beth took time for her
to interrupt her thoughts
to form and articulate something.
She spoke rarely at all, and when she did,
her speech was trembling and slow.
Beth was so quiet in her wheelchair
from her room to the dining hall,
hands folded and eyes cast downward.
One imagined what might be her thoughts.
She was so very quiet, downcast, and small.
The lesson of Beth is a difficult one,
she lived in a place so removed,
alive yet apparently so detached,
always poised as if in deep thought,
thoughts that she never did share,
perhaps simply waiting quietly to die.

I wonder if I were to live in such a place
as a crowded nursing home of the old,
always a part of a group, staff busy and behind,
rushing here and there with tasks.
How would I adjust to being here?
Would I speak and interact with folks,
or withdraw into myself like dear Beth?
Perhaps these are things I need to ponder,
today as I struggle for courage to fight
the downhill slide of my health.
Could I bear the sad surroundings
in a crowd of needy aged souls
or would I withdraw like silent Beth?

I think that my curiosity about people,
and my inclination to watch and wonder,
to learn important lessons from life,
would keep me quite happy, as I am today,
pondering folks like sweet quiet Beth.
There would be many folks I might ponder,
and capture in the soul of a poem.

January 2003

Grief

The pain of loss could torment me,
so many things I was able to do
have died and simply don't exist.
I can scream and rail at my losses.
I can try and fail endless times.
Neither my anger nor my courage
make those abilities return again.
They are gone forever in my life.

At times, I can become sad and distraught.
There is no joy or laughter in my losses.
Life can replay loss and intrude on today.
Life can smell like stale smoke in my being.

Always, one day, I become again curious about life.
Capabilities gone, but are there any I can explore?
I decide to commit to this search,
even if today I am able to find nothing.
With a new day, I might discover an ability.
This gives horizons for my hopes and dreams.
I might find ability I never knew I had.
I can develop the strength to try again.
I am creative and experiment with life.

Grace is never lost but dormant, awaiting discovery.
My life has darkness and also the hope of dawn.
Despite grief, life is always a wellspring of promise.

January 1995

Leslie Anne Miller

Smoke

I remember the old movies
when blowing smoke from
cigarettes into each other's eyes
was sexy and romantic
lending mystery to their lives.

A whole generation watched
and learned how blowing smoke
was dramatic and meaningful,
lending mystery to their lives.

Then, once addicted to smoke,
cigarettes became the villains,
no longer cool nor a fashion
lending mystery to their lives.

No, once addicted to smoke,
cigarettes, hard to put down,
caused blackened lungs and cancer
lending fewer years to those lives
and no mystery to their deaths.

No, once addicted to smoke,
cigarettes, hard to put down,
are tragic in their consequences
and a painful death to many lives.

No thank you, for a smoke,
take those cigarettes far away,
said people intently watching,
wiser by many painful losses,
adding years to their lives.

February 2003

Spring Cleaning

My kitchen junk drawer overflows with clutter,
exploding rubber bands and plastic closures,
flashlight batteries and dried up glue sticks,
pencils, scotch tape and broken drawer knobs.
Each time I open the drawer, I'm overwhelmed.

My kitchen junk drawer is like my life,
in need of a good spring cleaning.
I need to sort through confusion and debris
I have collected throughout the years.

Spring cleaning is a time for a renewal.
It's worthwhile to reorganize that junk drawer.
It's helpful to get rid of the
old angers that clutter up my life.
I'm ready to clean the cobwebs in my thinking.
It's appealing to make room for new life,
some new courage, new love, and new hope.

Spring cleaning will reward the focus and energy.
It's enough to clean one item, one day at a time.
Slowly, persistence will make it happen.
I don't have to be overwhelmed by this mess.
Spring cleaning is not larger than my abilities.
I can do it at my pace and with the energy I can muster.
There is enough time and reason for spring cleaning
to stop contemplating the messy task at hand.
Now where do find space to sort the mountain
that sprang from the junk drawer I opened?

May 1995

Leslie Anne Miller

Frost

It looks like a dusty sparkle
when the sun hits it just right,
frost signals a winter's arrival
and windshields needing to be scraped.

Frost changes the color of fall season
now dusted in a gentle coat of white.
Frost beckons the chill of winter
that will freeze the trees and brush.

What begins as a dusty sparkle
should be a signal in our lives,
that there might be a hint of a chill
and our life needs to be scraped.

Something altered what was our life
with a cold cover of pending change
that beckons forth a chilly fog
that winters our dated beliefs.

Seeing frost as a coat that sparkles,
yet warns of the winter ahead,
we expect to alter our journey,
melt frost and turn toward spring.
We need to listen to frosty warnings
that whispers the arrival of change
and hopes to enjoy a new spring.

February 2003

Dogs

She really wasn't much of a dog;
five and a half pounds of almost dog
made of scanty fringe on a squirrel frame.
Oh, but what a passionate busy body,
darting about squeaking her fury
at the heels of unwelcome strange shoes
daring to walk through her kitchen domain.

So much joy in such a little creature,
a lovable, sleepy fuzz ball nestled in my lap.

Pets and creatures don't care about problems,
rather food or some petting right now.

They remind us that love and affection
exist in all shapes and temperaments
even in a tiny busy body of a dog.

She was an endearing and healing tonic,
God's grace packaged quite small,
in feisty fuss-budget almost dog.

April 1995

Leslie Anne Miller

Easy Does It

I'm tired and worn out.
It's been a very long day.
I know that if I push, I will fail
and I'll find myself exhausted again.
I need rest to replenish my body and spirit.

It has been difficult to learn to stop
pushing myself beyond my abilities.
It was a time before I was willing to listen.
The world pushed at me with expectations.
It scolded me with endless comparisons
of appearance, energy and ability
and I felt like I was not enough.

Over the years, I discovered new paths
and a different way to move through life.
My leisurely pace is quite enough
on an alternate path through life.
I can relax, so I bend and not crack.
I am flexible, creative, and I explore.
I take time to notice the flowers of spring,
the rushed, the children and the old.
Ever so slowly, I have
learned an important lesson.

Easy does it,
that is enough,
and I am enough, too.

April 1995

Fudge

Oh, the sweet allurement of fudge,
with its chocolate slide so smooth,
down our willing gullets to taste,
the pleasure of fudge
in just the right place.

We know as we look upon fudge,
how weak our will power really is
when faced with the joyful taste
awaiting our melting resolve.

We know as we look upon fudge,
of the calories it spreads on hips,
but so wonderful a taste for lips,
we hope the spread will be small.

Fudge rules in my life, if it awaits
with its chocolate fragrance so sweet,
with taste so luxuriously smooth,
its beckoning too strong to resist.

I'm lucky I only invite that fudge
to enter my life on one occasion.
I make the sweet for young ones,
slim hips for its chocolate allure.

But once a year, when I make fudge,
I indulge and enjoy a fudge feast,
and the pleasure of warm fudge
in exactly the right place.

February 2003

Leslie Anne Miller

Humor

It's hard to see anything of joy in a loss.
Laughter can be a smoky turgidity,
a thin veil for insensitive denial.

Yet, humor can also empower strength,
and how warm the gentle light
of humor that reflects understanding
of the droll ironies of life's journey.

How easy it is to laugh
at what has been overcome,
remembering all the difficulty
in the light of the joy of recovery.

It is wonderful to laugh with someone
who has shared the courage of the journey.
And, it is courageous to laugh with someone
who genuinely struggles in their life.

Laughter gives dignity to our journey.

Laughter can be a touchstone on life's path.

Laughter can make troubles easier to bear.

God is the author of laughter
and sees the humor of our lives.

May 1995

Feet

Do you know of anyone who stops to think
of their gratitude for having two feet?
No, most folks take them for granted,
and instead think about all the accomplishments,
they need or want feet to obtain in their life.

Most folks awake to the marvel of feet
when after many years of use, they age
and create aches and pains and warts.
Even then, these feet are not loved.
Most folks ignore the problems of feet.

Were people able to appreciate their feet,
they would realize how lovely they are,
how balanced from front to back,
how strong in holding their weight.

Were they grateful for their trusty feet,
they'd know the miles they walked,
over many flat and hilly terrains,
over soft and hard surface types.

Were they grateful for the hard work of feet,
they'd think of the shoes they've worn
and their many years of service as feet.
They would not ignore their aged problems.
They would thankfully tend to their needs,
and shower them with comfort and ease,
to create motivation to carry their weight,
and take them where they want to walk.

Please people, have some gratitude for feet!

February 2003

Leslie Anne Miller

Owls, Eagles, and Hummingbirds

Owls in the trees observe the night,
eagles soar high in the skies by day,
hummingbirds flitter from flower to flower,
each is a very different type of bird.

These birds are a bit like people,
some who watch over us at night,
some who soar the skies in planes,
some who worry from problem to problem.

Such a celebration it would be,
if owls could join the eagles to soar,
and watch the earth as part of the flight,
Eagles could place a hummingbird
securely atop its wing,
so it could soar high for a moment,
to see a beautiful field of flowers.

Think how wonderful it is to imagine
that people appreciate the differences
between animals or people or trees,
all part of the mosaic, God created for us,
all interacting every day,
and all as different from each other
as are owls, eagles, and hummingbirds.

February 2003

Syrup

I have a love affair with syrup
in its many varied flavors to savor.
There's chocolate, perhaps my favorite,
especially hot fudge over ice cream,
and then sampled generously in large gulps.

Then, there is maple with its smell of trees,
dribbled slowly across my hot waffles,
and then sampled generously in large bites.

And there is honey with its smell of bees,
thick and spread lovingly on hot toast,
and sampled generously with a large crunch.

Also, there is blueberry and its smell of flowers,
thick and spread happily across pancakes,
and then sampled generously by the chomp.

There is butterscotch with its smell of butter,
poured willingly over more ice cream,
and then sampled generously by the spoon.

When I think about syrup, truth be told,
warm and thick, with its flavors and smells,
I dream about samplings of generous ladles,
syrups of different flavors and colors,
cascading into a sea of sweet delight,
my mouth awaiting a generous sample.

March 2003

Leslie Anne Miller

My House

Home is at the center of life's heart,
reflecting warmth, security, and love.

I have lived in many homes,
rooming houses, apartments,
a cabin and a trailer,
a "fixer upper," and a rock solid cottage.

Today, I think often of the home within me.
I've become aware that my home within
is a reflection of the home where I live.
I need look around my home
and ponder what it says about me.
Does it speak of inner clutter or order?
Does it speak of inner clatter or calm?
Does it speak of warm living or cold survival?
Does it speak of affection or dislike?
Does it reflect happiness or despair?
Is it secure or is it anxious?
Is it inviting or is it closed?

I'll take time to notice the home where I live
and learn more about my home within.
Perhaps I'll give my home a good cleaning
so the dust and grime are gone.
Perhaps I'll straighten the clutter and clatter
and create a quiet tranquil space.
Perhaps I'll redecorate it
and make my home more beautiful.
Perhaps I'll be more aware
of what I invite into my home
because within the home I live
is the home that I live within.

July 2002

Suffering Purpose

Today looms before me,
as a rugged mountain of struggle
demanding energy which is fleeting.
My body, quite leavened and sluggish,
fights valiantly to begin today's climb.

On those days, fatigue looms as my master.
It is hard to see the guiding hand of God.
What is God's purpose in this suffering?
Does my struggle inspire hope or fear?

When I'm exhausted, God teaches me
about being restful and relaxed,
things scarce in this busy culture.
The gifts that have been given me
become the gifts I have to give,
by the grace of God.

When I hurt, God gives me consolation.
I hurt and still paint.
I ache and still write.
I suffer and still sculpt.
The gifts that I have been given me
become the gifts I have to give,
by the grace of God.

When I suffer, God gives me love.
I suffer and love family.
I suffer and love friends.
The gifts I have been given me
become the gifts I have to give,
by the grace of God.

Leslie Anne Miller

When I am afraid, God gives me comfort.
I'm afraid and I walk slow.
I'm afraid and I listen.
I'm afraid and I pray.
The gifts that have been given me
become the gifts I have to give,
by the grace of a loving
and merciful God.

October 2001

Arthur

Arthur appreciated classical music
and a well-written book as well.
His bookshelf had been created
in a tiny walled off space
in a room he shared with another.

Most often, Arthur could be found there,
paging through a well-worn book,
listening to a beloved recording,
remembering better days of his life.

He could be coaxed out of his comfort
by a question about music or art.
His face would light up with pleasure,
sharing knowledge of his delight.
He was respected for his knowledge
and a cultural heritage held dear.

He loved to share a joke or two,
the more dastardly ribald the better,
a known secret of this cultured man.

Somehow, he knew all about the shock
that would come over someone's face
who knew him to be a man of fine art.
The contrasting joke, very dastardly ribald,
left them shocked in speechless bewilderment
while he loudly laughed with boisterous delight.

For those of us knowing the secret
of this proud and cultured man,
we'd watch as he took in a newcomer
with his books and music and art.
We would wait to hear his mischievous laugh
and we'd know the secret was out once again,
leaving a shocked look on someone's face
and Arthur loudly laughing in boisterous glee.

November 2002

One Link at a Time

My life is a link in a necklace of destiny.
When I inquire as to where my destiny lies,
I receive nothing but more questions
about something I cannot know.
Scaring myself with fearful links
is definitely a costly mistake.
Worry depletes the energy I have
to live my life well today
and to be the very best me.
I try to be the best link I can be
on the only day I have, which is today.
I can only live my life one link at a time,
discovering hidden links that are mine,
and then trusting that my life is well linked
with others in the necklace of life we share.
Link by link, my future is created
one day and one link at a time.
I can create a strong or a weak link
by choosing what link is possible,
a bold or a weak link, a large or a small link,
a round or a square link, a colorful or odd link,
all created one link at a time.
My life is linked in a necklace divine.

God sees the whole necklace I make of my life,
both sides, front and back at one time.
He sees the links of differing size,
strong or weak, large or small,
round or square, plain or beautiful,
the complete story of how I live my life.
My life is linked with other lives
in the grand necklace of our time.
God knows the color and shape of the links,
and how they create the final piece.
I need only remember that God is the artist.
I can only create a link that is my best
and understand life as well as I can.

God helps create my necklace if I let him,
with trust that it will be creative and lovely,
perhaps not a necklace that I understand,
but the necklace of mine that God created.
My life is linked in time with others
in the necklace of mankind.

November 2001

Happiness

The leaves are beginning to reflect
the golden hues of September,
the brilliant colors of fall that
arise out from the foliage of summer.
Children abandon their lemonade stands
to romp and frolic in the fall leaves.

Happiness arises out of appreciation
of life's seasons with their changing colors,
childhood games and adolescent crushes,
adult love and middle age comfort,
and finally aging wisdom.
Happiness arises out of appreciation
for the seasons of life as it evolves.

Happiness always begins with what I choose today.
I can focus on my suffering or my art that brings me joy.
I can focus on my pain or my new puppies.
I can focus on happiness which begins within me.

Prayer is a channel for God's happiness,
listening for his quiet and joyful voice within,
hearing His soft and loving voice without words,
appreciating all the wonder that is about me in life,
having gratitude for the gifts that I've been given.
There is no greater happiness than this.

God is the happiness that reminds me of heaven,
an eternal home I am longing to return to,
where happiness will be transformed into bliss.

November 2001

Endure

I hurt all over today.
I have no energy and I can't see to read.
I'm tired of struggling
and I feel discouraged and sad.

Yet, I know that I will endure
because I'm aware that each day is unique.
Some days, I hurt more and some days, I hurt less.
Some days, I'm not tired or discouraged or sad.

Some days, I notice the scarlet colors of fall
and I feel vibrant, happy, and alive.
Some days, I hear rain pelting the window
and I feel nourished, secure, and strong.
Always, I am so grateful for life,
for its people and lessons of love.

I can still love, and I'm still here.
I can still walk, and I can still reach.
I can still talk, and I can still hear.
I am grateful for little blessings in life.

So I hurt, and I live through it.
So I have no energy, and I live through it.
So I can't read, and I live through it.
Struggling, discouraged or sad,
I live through it.

My life is a stage of drama and contrast.
God has a purpose in this.
I remember the good when things are bad.
I appreciate the good because I remember the bad.

My drama is never boring.
There is always something to think about.
I endure because I love life.
Today is all I have
and it is a gift of God to have,
and that is enough.

November 2001

Affection

I adore the affection of my Yorkies,
all three, Bessie, Molly, and Zak.
They total 13.1 lbs of rascal critters
that warm and nourish my spirit.

Zak leaps at my knee with his "barbell,"
two balls appearing either side of his mouth,
nudging and pawing my heels to the door,
then beckoning me back to let him in.
When I open the door he runs off again,
turning to tease from across the yard.

Bessie bullies Molly, and Molly bullies Bessie
before they snuggle together on soft pillows.
Zak basks in his great romance with Molly,
showing his passion with vigor and force.

Somehow, each day there is a new drama
as the three of them snuggle and chase
the many squirrels that scamper the yard.

I adore also the affection of my sweetheart.
Its warmth gently nourishes my soul.
Its strength shown daily through small things,
my spoon always there on my place mat
with sweet oranges cut on a plate,
warm hugs to awaken and drift to asleep,
loving memories that lift my spirit.

I enjoy my friends at lunch with a chat,
each chat forging friendships more dear.

Affection is a transforming and healing gift.
Affection connects our spirit to the moment.
Affection is love, energy, and life.

Suffering is eased by affection.
Burdens are lightened by affection.
Souls are graced by affection.

God is an affectionate God.
Thank God.
And I do.

November 2004

Leslie Anne Miller

Anger and Hatred

Anger can burn hot in relationships
or channeled into commitment for change.

Hatred burns caring to cinders and ashes
because hatred is deep anger smoldering,
glowing dark, and full of wrath.

Anger is a human emotion that comes and goes.
It can be channeled to something good.
With hated, there are feelings of searing pain
that can burst into a fire of rage.

The challenge of hatred is to rekindle
some perspective and understanding.
Cooling the cinders of hatred
takes time, commitment, and courage.

The passion of hatred need not overcome
the passion of courage and persistence.

Out of anger can come caring and healing.
Out of hatred can come understanding and peace.

Anger and hatred are no match for courage.
Anger and hatred are no match for change.
Anger and hatred are no match for new life,
relationships of understanding perspective.

November 2001

Quiet Wisdom

Today is a sunny serene kind of day.
I awoke feeling very quiet and thoughtful
which guided me to a tranquil place within.

Once there, I discovered a connection with myself
that I was unaware of in my busy time of life.

The beginning of wisdom evolves from this quiet.
Wisdom returns to the quiet for its growth.
Reflection is a path to our inner wisdom,
a journey for connection with self and God.

Today allows peace to arise from the quiet,
which leads to a place of sacred connection.

Wisdom quietly seeps within me from this journey.
Taking time for sacred journeys reflects wisdom.

December 1996

Leslie Anne Miller

What Not to Believe

Television equates beauty with youth,
success with accomplishment and wealth
and health as personal achievement.
My culture has beliefs that diminish me
as a person struggling to cope with loss.

I am not beautiful.
I lost my career to disability and retired.
My youth, health, and ability are departing.

I have to choose what to believe very carefully.
I have to choose thoughtfully what not to believe.

The values of my culture are not helpful to me
because those values do not reflect who I am.
I now see beauty as spiritual,
success as serenity and peace,
and health as a grace from God.

I choose what not to believe in my culture.
I now see worth as integrity,
career as vocation,
and personal achievement as spiritual growth.

It is important to consider what to believe
and what not to believe.
God guides my choices,
if I choose to let him.

God inspires me to be more than I think I am.
God inspires me to be more
than my culture thinks I am.
And, with God's help, I am
all God intended me to be
and each day, I let him guide me home.

November 2001

Art

Art teaches about life
through an artist's unique lens.

I am late to know I am an artist and
late to know I have always been one.
It took painful losses to retire my career.
It took the grace of God
to awaken the artist within me.

Art is creation.
Art is imagination.
Art is expression
in many aspects and forms,
some conventional, some expansive,
all a unique contribution
to creative thought.

As I look back,
I see my artistry hidden in busyness,
achievement, and career.
I see my artistry hidden in shadow.

An artist with painful loss has a unique lens
that is colored by suffering and longing
and colored by possibility,
inspiration, meaning, and hope.

Now, I envision my life as a mosaic.
Today is a flicker of color or shade,
warm or cool, in sun or shadow.

Tomorrow's moment is hidden in uncertainty.
Yet, tomorrow I'll still be an artist
despite painful loss and inabilities.

And always, always there will be art.

November 2002

Leslie Anne Miller

Pain and Hope

My body hurts,
my thoughts are weary,
my legs are like leaden logs.
When I think of a day in my life,
I want for a day off from it.
There are no days off from my life.

As today looms before me,
I imagine it a trying marathon.
Before my day has even started,
I have scared myself about beginning.
I'm aware it's an easy pathway from fear
to neglect, disuse, and disability.

Then, I imagine today a leisurely stroll
that beckons me one step at a time.
I imagine today a gentle healing
of hurts and fatigue and fears.
Reassured, I muse, why not use
the ability and courage I have
to imagine some moments of joy?

A moment to imagine isn't fearful.
It's also a pause from thinking about pain.
A moment to imagine is a breath of life.
It can also be a gift of joy or hope.
A moment of hope captures another and another.
Hope inspires gentleness, kindness, and peace.
A moment of hope eases pain.
It is enough of a grace to believe in grace
and grace is my shepherd through the day.

I choose a moment
to imagine God is a good friend
walking quietly here beside me.
Leaning on His compassion, I find the courage
to begin the journey of today,
confident I'll handle the challenge of pain
and excited about the day's possibilities
for finding moments of joy and hope.
It is a moment of imagined possibility
and that is enough for today.

September 2002

Leslie Anne Miller

Bicycles

Two wheeled marvels of my childhood,
they transported me through my youth,
from exploring the hilly neighborhood,
to zipping across campus to class.

I thought I'd left them in my childhood
as memories old and fine.
Today, I'm without balance to ride
those two wheeled childhood prides.

Then one day, I remembered again,
the three wheeled beginning I had,
the tricycle that began my love affair
with those bicycles swift and sleek.

By gosh, I discovered tricycles exist
for aging adults like me.

With time to explore the small neighborhood,
made smaller the frailer my legs,
I found a tricycle that I could ride
the one street my frail legs could master.
Oh, the laughter and glee coasting the street
with wind in my hair, moments of wonder
and new memories of a street well traveled.
It delights me every time I dare take the time
to venture out on my beloved tricycle!

March 2003

Noise

The roar of the city always drowns out
the muted rustle of leaves in my yard.

Another car alarm screeches.
Another aircraft thunders.
The freeway grumbles and groans,
bloated with rush hour traffic.

The noise pushes with angry shoves,
intruding in on my spirit,
shattering, splintering, and injuring.
The noise without becomes the noise within.
My spirit becomes dormant and hidden.

Noise fuels my search for quiet within,
a search that wanders
and stretches to reach,
a search that grasps
and captures my spirit.

This search takes some time,
rare on culture's fast track.
The search takes some risk
to be more than I think I am.
The search takes commitment
to be my best self and more.

When there is time to really consider,
to listen and quietly ponder
the muted rustle of my thoughts
gently flowing through the quiet,
it is here where I find my joy
and the quiet within is then able
to protect my spirit from noise.

To cultivate noise or spirit is a choice.
Spirit needs time and quiet.
Noise needs haste and chatter.
I choose to cultivate my spirit
in order that I can become
more than I think I am,
and all God intended me to be.

March 2002

Leo

Leo was a crusty and feisty fisherman,
who might growl when greeted each day,
or perchance on a whim, his eyes might twinkle
and a slight smile would start on its way.

One never knew which reaction would ensue,
so greeting Leo was a risk.
Yet it was worth it to greet him anyway,
for everyone sensed he did like it.

Whether growling or twinkling,
well, no one ever really knew.
It was fun to lay bets on the day
as to which reaction would ensue.

I think of Leo years later on occasion
and a lesson I learned from him.
It mattered less what his reaction was,
than that he was greeted everyday.

It mattered more to try to connect
because it told a guy like Leo why
he was special enough to be cared about,
enough to risk a growl on any given day.

November 2002

Leslie Anne Miller

Darkness and Light

My world grows smaller and darker.
Losses abound.
Pain has a grip.
Connections are broken.
Fabric is unraveled.
Places and activities are lost.
Where is the light of hope?

Always, there will be darkness.
Hope whispers that there will be light.
The light of faith opens to possibility.
Faith rekindles hope; the hope of opportunity.

Yes, there are many places I cannot go,
and, there are still places that I can go,
places unknown I have yet to discover.
Yes, there are things I can no longer do.
And, there are things I have yet to try.

Faith tends to embolden hope
to seek light within the dark,
perhaps a tiny light for the search.
I do what I can and let the rest go.
I look forward to life's discovery.

Hope brings light that dispels the dark.
so we can see God's endless possibilities.
It's an important gift of God to cultivate.

Hope.

June 2003

Fairy Tales

Oh, the stories that young children are told
of a prince handsome, dashing, and bold,
who rescues the princess with beauty and grace,
from life's most darkened and terrifying place.

Oh, the stories that children are told
and believed as attainable truths of life.
They dream of being a handsome prince
or a beautiful princess with grace.
They dream of rescue from life's rough trials,
the rescues of a princess from harm.

With dreams such as these, fed to them young,
is it not surprising little girls often wonder
if they have the beauty to attract that prince
who will save them from problems in life?
Or, is handsome and dashing required of each prince?
Or, a search in life for a graceful princess
to save her from the distress life has in store?

Oh, the stories that young children are told
and believed as attainable truths of life.
They were fooled and their dreams were not,
no prince or princess have they become.
We need be more careful
what we spoon feed our young,
these fairy tales planted
deep in young minds.

March 2003

Leslie Anne Miller

Pretense

I recognize my pretense.
It is my independence, surviving without help,
which I thought was necessary to be an adult.
It is a luxury, the illusion of independence.

We are dependent on parent's genetics
and on parent's experience to guide us.
We are dependent on teachers' knowledge,
and on the role models we receive in life.
We are dependent on God's grace
whether we believe in grace or not.

When we age and our health fails,
this illusion crumbles and
our pretense lies in ashes.
Out of the ashes of pretense and illusion,
wisdom can emerge and truth can be learned.

Our lives are interconnected and intertwined.
We need one another.
We are not alone.
We cannot stand alone in life.

That is the truth, the reality behind pretense
and reality is what we need to be adult.

July 1995

Solitude

Solitude is a healing balm for my spirit,
an inner journey to the quiet within me.
There, I find a spiritual bond with the world.
There, I know I am small yet an integral part of life.
There, I realize the world is a living breathing organism
of which I am a part.
Solitude can strengthen the spirit.

There are those who dislike being alone.
They experience solitude as a stinging brine.
Their spirit connects in the company of others.
Spirituality is a journey unique to each person.

How sad to label those who seek solitude
as deviant or lacking in love.
How sad to discount someone's journey
toward a spiritual bond with the world.

Let me honor solitude to connect with life,
and let me honor those
who need the company of others.
Let me connect with people who respect
and honor each other's spiritual path.
Whether in solitude or company,
we are connected to one another
in spirit.

November 2002

Mary

She sat heaving her breathing, quite tiny,
connected to a large noise machine
which weighed even more than her 54 lbs,
it standing 3' tall to her 5'4".
Our eyes met when I walked past her room
on the critical wing that day,
we both knew in that instant
that we knew each other well.
How I knew that was beyond me.
I just knew that it was true.

The first time I visited her room,
there was a huge transformation in me.
I had never been in a place like this,
that had so much peace, calm, and joy,
like we were sitting by a bubbling brook
where time and space were suspended.
It felt like this must be like heaven,
Mary, with that monster machine.
And I knew there was no other place on earth
that I'd rather be that day.
I just wanted to be near Mary
and her peace and her joy and her way.

I'd visit each day and bring magazines
with pictures of animals and birds,
the language we had was gestures,
because we had no words.
She showed me her life in the village,
and taught me the sewing of mukluks,
and how whale was sliced and prepared
and how wonderfully delicious it was.

Across the dinning room, large as it was,
I'd catch her eyes cast down,
then looking up suddenly, intent on me,
saying silently across the huge room,
"How can I enjoy this slimy spaghetti,
and how might you like some raw whale?"

One night as I finished my chart notes,
and I looked out into the hallway,
Mary was clinging to the hall guard rail,
having walked two hallways to find me.
I was in a terrible state of dismay,
as I called to the charge nurse to say,
"Please get a wheelchair for Mary,
before she collapses to the floor."

In the wheelchair, I said to Mary,
"I come to see you each day I'm here,
you don't need to come find me."
She looked up at me quite intently,
with her quiet and huge soulful eyes.
There was something she had come to say,
and so it was important to come this way.
"This I give you," she said in a whisper,
clasping firmly my nerve wracked hands.
She had come to bring me a ceramic frog,
a gift I really didn't understand.

That Sunday while I was eating dinner,
some twenty miles away,
I felt and heard her distress in my head
though I knew she was a distance away.
She was dying in agony in my mind for a moment.
Then suddenly, there was peace and calm,
like the quiet joy of the first day we met,
only now instead of walking to her room,
her presence was strong inside my head.

I have no good explanation of why it is true
that Mary is with me, at times, these years later,
her presence is often a question to me,
"Why are you allowing this stress?"
Her presence says that our relationship is true,
with the amazing bond we have held,
all else is simply distracting noise
that fills our lives to the brim
so that there is no room for connection
and no time for relationship to bloom.
I am grateful I have known Mary
and I know it's important that I share
the connection that happened between us
and continues these decades still there.
It happened because we nourished the bond
and gave it time and patience to flower.
These bonds are much more important
than the lives of cacophony we power.

December 2002

Freedom

I sometimes feel imprisoned in my body
and in moments like this I remember
that the price of freedom is struggle,
even as exhausting and draining as today.

The price of freedom from pain is hope
even in the face of discouragement.
The price of freedom from pain is resolve
to seek out the possibility of its relief.
The price of freedom from pain is courage
even in the face of difficulty.

Nothing can imprison my spirit.
It struggles to be strong and free,
despite the shackled body I have,
I know God gives me the gift of life.

The spirit's freedom is in letting go
and letting God take full charge
of what my life purpose might be.
The God of my spirit is without limits.
Freedom is letting go and let God
expand my world of possibilities.

Freedom is living in God
and trusting in the journey
of the life that He has given me.

November 2001

Race Car

He was fine to behold speeding along
experiencing his life
with both hands and both feet
like the fine race car that he was.
Why he took an interest in me,
I don't know because I traveled slow,
and he was capable of such speed.

Yet, soon we were a team, he and me,
speeding through life,
really not knowing
what life would behold together.
Once hitched, I was dragged,
speeding much too fast for me
and he was tethered to a car
that was much too slow for him.

It was hard to admit
that we were happier apart,
he racing
and I strolling through life.
It was hard to detach,
to say good-bye and let go,
but that's what caring demanded.

Today, he is whizzing through life
teamed with faster race car,
speeding off toward his destiny.
And I stroll along peacefully,
with a slower yet steady partner.
I'm happy with the quiet pace of my journey,
and with memory of that fine race car.

November 2002

Puppets and Heroes

I'm hostage again to suffering and loss,
a puppet with tangled strings,
and I stumble, collide and fall.
I feel so crumpled and broken,
and I'm unable to see my way
beyond the strangled heap of mind and body.
I could spend my life snarled in immobility;
how easy to feel intimidated by the effort
that it always takes to stand upright again.

At moments like these, I remember my heroes,
people who struggled beyond pain and sorrow
to achieve greatness of spirit and soul.
Their courage to rise again and again,
emboldens my inner grit,
a gift of my father raised in the streets.
If they can rise above suffering and loss,
then using my grit, so can I.

Ascending from a knotted heap
will take time,
tenacity and hope, spirit and mind.
Today, I won't shrink from the challenge.
Rather, I will fasten my mettle and mind
to the hope of my heroes' paths
to guide me surely out of the dark,
remembering the hope of the rise,
remembering celebration and joy,
a precious gift from my sweet mother,
imagining the endless possibilities
of rising from a tangled heap.
I know from my parents' strong grit and joy,
I will rise to the challenge of life
and persist to be all that God wants me to be,
more than I think I am,
and
that is enough for me.

December 2002

Leslie Anne Miller

Winter

A winter storm aptly describes
the painful times in my life.
Loss and grief blew in with dark fury.
It seemed the storm would never end,
and that the morning would never come.
Finally, when the fierce storm did end,
my life was limp in exhaustion and pain.

It was a while until I noticed life again.
It took longer to see the rainbows,
rainbows of hope for the future.
It took longer to notice hush in my soul.
So much I thought important was just noise.
Loss became the snow that dampened the noise.
Loss created the time to seek quiet in my soul.

Loss and grief are a long winter storm
that blankets my life and quiets the din.
Loss and grief hunger for peace within.
Rainbows, however tiny, give my life hope
and hope is a powerful healer of wounds.

The winter storm has passed.
Morning has again arrived.
The cold air tickles my nose as I breathe.
Frost coats the trees in layered crystal dust,
sparkling their vibrant rainbows in the sun.
The noise of the city is softly dampened
and a soft snow blanket quiets the din.
Peace, at long last has seeped within me
where the loss and grief had stormed in.

September 1997

Gib

Gib was a man of some importance,
a cowboy hatted past president
of the Geological Association.
He always arrived late for the class,
interrupting the group as he entered,
and needing help to remove his sling
to begin his arm's range of motion.
Day after day this was his ceremony
of entering the room in his great style,
thriving on having the rest of the group wait
for his royal readiness to join in.

One day one of the group members,
a blunt spoken woman named Bernice,
could not stand the wait any longer
without speaking her mind at least.
"Oh, Gib, you just want the attention
that's why you arrive here so late."
"Well," Gib replied with poise in his voice,
"If you only knew how much I hurt."
With that, he wanted his sling back on
so he could leave the room with his dignity,
and leave he did, wheeling out to the hall
where Gib quietly died that day.

When Bernice learned of Gib's demise,
so close to where he had left the group,
she decided that she had caused his death
with her comment so brisk and unkind.
Because of painful feelings in the group,
we talked a long while about Gib
and the fact that a single comment
could not be the cause of a demise.

Leslie Anne Miller

Still, there was a lesson there that I learned.
Since we can't know the hour of our demise,
unkind words could be the last words spoken
in a relationship between two people.
It behooves us to remember this thought
as we interact with people in our lives.
So, Gib remains in my memory these many years later.
I'm quite sure that our Gib, now in heaven,
still sports his grand hat and demeanor.

November 2002

Advice

Advice is sometimes appreciated,
especially when someone asks.
Advice is sometimes resented,
especially when no one asked.

No matter the topic or importance,
no matter how difficult to withhold,
advice is something to consider;
it is important that someone ask.

So, the next time one is tempted
to offer a bit of sage advice,
it's better to ask if it's welcomed,
or if their own counsel is preferred.

Advice is a tricky business,
and is an important thing as well,
one that can be appreciated,
when allowing freedom to decide
whether it is welcome or not.

Advice can be something that honors.
Advice can show a lack of respect.
Thus, it is very important to honor
the importance of freedom of choice,
the importance of freedom of thought,
the importance of freedom of time
to figure things out for ourselves.

February 2002

Leslie Anne Miller

Closed Doors

I stared at life's doors that slammed shut,
a knot in my throat, tears swollen within.
How could this happen? Why me, Lord?
What quality of life is possible now?

Ripped away were huge chunks of my life;
having children, going to work,
having energy to leave my home.
It ripped at the flesh of my soul.
There were doors in my life that closed
and I pounded against them in wild fury.

Worn by my rage, bruised and weary,
finally there was time and healing.
I accepted my fate and then asked the question,
what possibilities exist in my life?
What lessons was my life trying to teach me?
Slowly, as I learned the lessons of my life,
I discovered there were open windows.

My life is quiet now, and teaches me contemplation.
My physical abilities wax and wane
as my spirit learns how to soar.
The wounds of my struggle
find the healing of compassion.
I have emerged still very much alive.
I am strong, vibrant, and whole
just the way I am.
My soul finds new depth from surviving losses.

An opportunity for growth arose from despair.
There were lessons arising from rage.
With the grace of God,
hope can emerge from the devastation of loss
and creates new possibilities to explore
and new lessons in living life fully alive.

September 1997

Sexuality

Sex seeps and gushes from television,
sexuality of the young, thin, and beautiful.

It leaves me disgusted and repulsed.
Television portrays sexuality
as simply an act of intercourse,
not an act of love with commitment.
TV sex is about separation, not union.
It demonstrates attraction, not love.
It reflects appearance, not spirit.

In spirit, sexuality is part of my being,
part of who I am with my mate through the day.
Together, it is making our bed in the morning,
reading editorials and sharing thoughts,
sharing quiet dinners, letting the dogs out,
watching the sunset, gazing at stars.

Sexuality is a joining of souls.
It is sharing both sorrow and laughter.
It reaches great heights and finds new depths.

Commercial sexuality is puddles.
Loving sexuality is the ocean.
Careless sexuality is joining bodies not souls.
Mature sexuality is joining souls and bodies.

March 1999

Leslie Anne Miller

Floating

Disability interrupted the flow of my life.
I felt angry at inability and inadequacy.
I tried to return to my former self.

I insisted on swimming upstream.

It was a time of despair and failure.
I persisted with things I could no longer do.
People became angry at their inability to help.
My despair became theirs.
We suffered our connection.

Unbearable suffering left me weary.
Endless weary left me searching.
Searching left me changed.

I have learned to do the things I can do.
I learn the lessons of life today.
I have grown a new view of myself.
I trust God and follow His stream,
home to the ocean of His love.

People express joy at their ability to help.
My learning and success become theirs.
We celebrate our connection.

I have learned to float the stream of my life
trusting God with the direction
that leads me home.

March 1999

Wings

Birds have wings that take them high,
soaring through the clouds.
So high they fly, they seem to try
to wing so high, they touch the sky.

Bats have wings that fly at night
through darkened sky and cave.
They fly so odd they seem to try
to frighten us and make us cry.

Bees have wings that fly to flowers
tasting with sweet caress.
That they fly at all with bodies round
is a mystery still of science profound.

Angels have wings that fly unknown
through our lives and yonder beyond.
They fly so high beyond the sky
to wing so high they make us sigh.

Does life have wings, we know not where?
Can it fly so high we're unaware
that life really can fly at all,
or that it has the power to bring us
close to touch an angel's wing?
If it is true, my oh my,
my life might touch the sky
and I need not ponder why.

God's creation surrounds us
to discover, celebrate and live fully.

March 2003

Leslie Anne Miller

Love and Mourning

Love's sweet essence lingers in my mind
when love is not gone but lost.
Though death may take, love goes on,
still sweet, still eternal, still strong.

Love strengthened by years is a lioness,
not frightened by death's stolen grasp.
Love strengthened by years is a lion,
not panicked by death's cold caress.

Love's sweet essence lingers in the soul,
a soul that is protected from above.
Though death may take, love goes on,
still sweet, still eternal, still strong.

Love's sweet essence is a part of the being
of a person that has loved for years.
Though death may take, love goes on,
still sweet, still eternal, still strong.

We mourn the loss of physical touch,
sweet glance, strong presence, and song.
Love's sweet essence is part of the soul,
sweet soothing for a journey's sorrow.

February 2003

Stew

Stew is rather like people,
different colors and shapes,
flavors and textures,
all mixed together
with the sauce of life.

People are rather like stew,
some shaped like potatoes,
some carrots or peppers,
some onions or chives,
all mixed together
with the sauce of life.

Think of the flavor of stews
some with more onions,
some with more chives,
some with more leaves,
some with more peppers,
all mixed together
with the sauce of life.

I rather like different stews,
and I rather like different people,
all mixed together
with the sauce of life.

February 2002

Leslie Anne Miller

Worms

Consider the life of the lowly worm,
crawling deep within the earth,
and occasionally across the ground,
its life is mostly making tunnels in dirt,
helping flowers grow deep in the ground.

Though most don't think of the slippery worm
and the important work it provides,
they do think of their colorful flowers,
and take credit for the worm's handiwork.

But whoever compliments the earthly worm,
making dirt loose so plant roots can grow,
and hidden under the soil of the flowers,
unappreciated for a lifetime of work.

Worms provide food for the birds
that wait for them to appear from their dirt,
and worms provide good food for fish,
whenever dangled as bait from a hook.

So I, for one, want to say to all worms,
"I appreciate all the work that you do
for the flowers that you help to grow,
for the food you are for birds and fish.
Thank you, worms, for all of your good work.

February 2003

Meetings

I think of all the meetings we have
through the course of a single day,
we meet at breakfast with loved ones,
our traffic companions and coworkers,
the secretary, janitor or maid.

As we go about our single day,
do we think about how we meet
with the people along the way?

Do we begin our day with an argument
then continue with angry traffic yells,
are we distant with our coworkers,
oblivious of the janitor
and not aware of the grocery clerk?

Wouldn't it be wonderful to start a day
with a smile and hug and loving gaze,
with patience and generosity in traffic,
positive greetings and cooperation at work,
a hi and a hello to the janitor,
a smile to our laden grocery checker,
and "thank you" sprinkled through the day?

Meetings are quite important encounters.
They are the very substance of our lives.
There, we can leave a reflection of caring
for the people we meet during our day.

If we greeted with warmth the people
that we encounter throughout the day,
we might return home feeling much better
about ourselves and the varied people
we encounter through any one day.

It's the little gestures we give to each other
that build the relationships we need in life.
Meeting people with thoughtful greeting
and consideration of their roles in life
might soften the world we experience
and how we feel when we get home at night.

February 2003

Adversity

Adversity can be grim, dark, and difficult.
Getting through adversity can create
cynicism and anger, rigidity and despair.

Adversity can be ugly, harsh, and dangerous.
Getting through adversity can also inspire
courage and creativity, values and faith.

Adversity can be a wound, raw and bleeding.
Getting though adversity often produces
strength and toughness, determination and grit.

Adversity can sear, sever, and scar.
Getting though adversity can also bring
flexibility and calm, perspective and wisdom.

What we bring to adversity,
what we allow of adversity,
is what we can bring from adversity.
Ourselves and our destiny.

March 2003

Leslie Anne Miller

Rain

My heart sinks when the forecast
is for weather of gray clouds and rain.
The gloom of rain in this rainy city
is gray sky on gray black concrete.

At times, my heart sings when the forecast
is for weather of gray clouds and rain.
The pleasure of rain near the ocean
is gray sky on a vast forest of green.

Not happy with a heart that sinks,
in a city with many forecasts of rain,
I've discovered that when I create a fire,
the fireplace spreads its warm glow
and the fire is dancing colored flames.

So, when my heart sinks at the forecast,
for a dark city of gray clouds and rain,
it only sinks for a brief moment of time
until I remember the warm glow of a fire.

So, today I'm happy here in the city,
with weather of gray clouds on concrete.
And, I'm happy when I travel to the ocean
with weather of gray rain on green forest.

Being happy whatever the forecast
applies to the rest of my journey,
whether I have gloom or doom or glee,
my happiness is in what I choose to see,
and that makes all the difference.

March 2003

Bugs

They have short and long and many legs
as they crawl about in the garden,
which is the place where bugs belong.
When I see one race about in my bathtub,
I cringe at the task that is at hand,
to capture the racing bathtub bug,
taking care to not squash it in the process,
then walking the hostage racing bug,
back to crawl in the soil of the garden,
which is the place where all bugs belong.

The hardest types of bugs to capture
are those that fly everywhere at once,
about my clean kitchen, resting on windows,
somehow knowing they belong outdoors,
trying to fly out the window to the garden,
which is the place where these bugs belong.
I have to wait until the bug tires and rests
for a moment on a near window pane,
and not so very high I'm unable to reach
to capture the exhausted resting bug
and gently take it back to the garden
which is the place where bugs do belong.

The truth be known I rather like little bugs,
when they are not crawling about in my house,
rather they need to crawl about in the garden,
which is the place where all bugs belong.

April 2003

About Leo

It was something about his gruff response,
speaking hushed in just a single syllable,
and his slow mighty effort to turn toward you
so he could look you squarely in the eye.
It was something about his gravelly low voice
and his general annoyance at an interruption
from thinking seriously about who knows what.

Leo fought bravely in his long last struggle
to manage the effort of another day.
There was his enormous struggle to move
to get dressed for a day of his life
then undressed for yet another night.
There was the struggle to put food on his fork
and then raise it as high as his mouth.
There was the struggle to maintain his dignity,
as he sat in his chair most of the day.
With much time and a great tiring toil,
he would for reach the wheel of his chair
and move it along slowly like a turtle
for a few yards before he grew tired.

Leo sat strong in his stiffness each day,
mostly alone in his chair with his thoughts,
interrupted on occasion by greetings from staff
scurrying about the busyness of their day.
He would slowly attempt to respond to them
with a gruff gravel greeting of his own
that had a fondness attached to its tone.
It was then that there was an opportunity
to let him know that he was admired
for his brave struggle to live out each day.
It was then that Leo might actually believe
that the admiration conveyed was sincere.
And only then would a slow smile appear.

I remember Leo with great fondness today,
so brave and strong in his long struggle.
He inspires me today in my tough moments
when, truth is, I'm not feeling all that brave.
I think of Leo and how courageous he was
and I'm inspired and know his courage helps me.
Often I thank him for the slow smiles we shared
that are preserved in my memory to this day.

March 2003

Leslie Anne Miller

Computers

I have days when the urge is overwhelming
to send my stubborn computer to the fate it deserves.
I'd throw it out the window with the keyboard.
Then the printer and monitor would be warned.

Whether or not my computer behaves
depends more on its mood and the weather today,
than any rational reason I can think of.

The madder I get, the worse its revenge.
It can stop all functioning for days on end.
My only revenge is to ignore it as it sits there,
after the computer has taken my e-mail hostage.
Then humbled, I make my insincere apology
and pay homage to this dratted machine.

Though I need the computer to write my poems,
and to correspond with my friends,
I know if it realizes my true feelings about it,
the dratted computer will seek its revenge.

So the computer and I have an unhappy truce,
I am gentle with the keys and look kindly at the screen.
Truth be known if it acts up again, I will scream.
But machines don't listen too well, it's true.
But they'd feel the impact of a very long fall,
and I can often imagine that revenge after all.

April 2003

River, Waterfall, and Sea

Rain replenishes the water that flows
from the river to waterfall to the sea,
a journey of life for the fish to swim
and a journey of creation for the river
carving its path as it seeks out the sea.
It is a journey of crashing cacophony,
roaring over vast cliffs in a waterfall
that moves a large river toward the sea.

God replenishes the soul that flows
from growth to challenge to wisdom.
It's a journey of life for our experience
and a journey of creation for the soul
carving its path as it seeks wisdom.
It's a journey of cacophony as it splashes
over challenges through crisis to thoughts
toward growth and then finally wisdom.

God replenishes the soul that flows
from growth to challenge to wisdom.
It's a journey of life and creation,
the wisdom of returning to God.

May 2003

Leslie Anne Miller

The Value of a Nose

The nose is an important gift that
most faces are lucky to have.
They add some interest to the face
being pug or roman, or flat,
being thin or squared or round.

The nose is an important gift to have.
It's job not well known by most
who think of other things than their nose.

The nose has an important function,
breathing fresh air into the lungs,
filtering air from harmful bacteria,
as well as particles, smoke, and fumes.

The nose has the primary function
for smelling our bacon and eggs.
The nose smells food and helps us taste
the fragrant dishes on our dinner plates.

So when you look into the mirror today
to wash your face or brush your teeth,
take a moment to notice that you have a nose,
and appreciate that you have one that works!

July 2003

Grit

It was easy to know where to find him,
behind the paper or watching television,
recovering from the stress of his day at work
selling complex investments to skeptical people
on a straight commission basis of pay.
He was an introvert in an extrovert career,
and he needed to put food on a table for six.

It was the grit of a depression survivor,
who had no father to guide him as a child
or put food on his youth's table of five,
and who shot pigeons in the park for a meal.
He also had a tattoo on his left upper arm
with a grand display of a large floral heart,
bannered by the name of a teenage love.
He didn't realize then that tattoos last for life
or that one future day he would marry someone
with a very different name than his arm.
He didn't yet know his wife named Virginia
would sleep with this large floral heart,
its banner displaying the name of Lorraine
for the thirty-four years of their marriage.

It was the grit of a depression survivor,
growing up with no father to guide him,
as to how exactly to be a good father,
to a noisy active brood of four children.
Of some things, he knew for a certainty,
having run wild in the streets as a child,
a child should not do whatever they want,
or be allowed to go wherever they please.
A good father should lay down the law,
mostly expressed with a loud abrupt "NO,"
from which children fled to their mother,
who was also a depression survivor,
yet had a fondness for the happy word "yes,"
if no one would be harmed or burdened.

It was the grit of a depression survivor,
who grew up with no father to guide him,
alone in the living room from his children,
because of the paper, TV and loud "NO,"
who always was committed to his children,
guarding fiercely in his frame of armor,
this lively family of wife and kids,
no matter not knowing exactly how.
He maintained the cars, house, and lawn
and stayed the course in his role of father.
The father that he never had himself
was the father that he intended to be.

It was the grit of a depression survivor,
growing up with no father to guide him,
that long after his life was over,
inspired one of his four adult children
to write a poem about beloved Dad.

No matter his stern style of fatherly love,
it was his steel commitment and grit.
One always knew where to find him,
and knew that he would never leave,
and that he tried his best to love them,
by providing and maintaining a home.
Without having a father to guide him
he was the good father he intended to be.

I realize now, decades later after his death,
that despite the paper, TV, and loud "NO,"
it was the grit of this depression survivor,
having had no father to guide him,
who modeled a life of commitment,
discipline, fortitude, and love of reading,
a legacy his children possess today.

It was the grit of a depression survivor,
growing up with no father to guide him,
who was the good father he intended to be,
and is much missed, remembered, and loved.

In memory of Dad.

March 2003

Crows

Oh, the plight of those poor black crows,
    that venture today toward our car,
after my husband has washed it with care.
He shakes his mighty fist in fury at them.

    "You blasted black crows,
      stay away from my car
      that I lovingly washed today,
      don't you dare to venture near it,
    I'm warning you. Do you hear me?"

Well, the crows do see his angry stance.
    after washing his car with great love.
Just when he is safely nowhere to be seen,
they make sure to have a visit with his car.

"Why MY car, you blasted black crows?
Find another clean car, do you hear me?"
and he shakes his fist to demonstrate his ire.
    They wait again until he has safely left,
    to make certain they visit HIS clean car.

I see those black crows watching on high,
    as he shakes his fist again in robust fury,
    they enjoy the game of his mighty fist,
and waiting around to visit HIS clean car.

                    May 2003

Baseball

"Well, how are you, Nancy, in coping with your MS,
that makes energy and walking such a struggle?"

"Well, I'm OK I guess, but it's hard to find help,
I've been waiting on my helper to go to the store.
Sometimes she is late, or doesn't come at all,
leaving me waiting for her all day.
I can't get the things done that I need to do."

"Nancy, how's baseball, are you listening to the games
on the portable radio that you carry?"
Nancy is transformed, she sits up straight,
her eyes glistening and her face all aglow.
"Well, there's a game today, I won't miss,
though last night they lost four to one.
It's really sad that they're going to lose
that fine pitcher who will be leaving soon."

I love the transformation of Nancy
at the mere mention of a baseball game.
Despite the struggles she daily endures,
she is an impassioned and devoted fan.
MS affects Nancy but never touches baseball.

February 2003

Moonlight

The light of the moon is majestic
as it shimmers on water and trees,
as it glistens across mountain snow,
or beckons through grey buildings,
or brightens the darkened night sky.

Moonlight is a quiet hush,
a gentle reflection of radiance,
a muted expanse of brilliance,
a soft glow adorning the sky.

In the moonlight of my life,
the sun has set, the dusk is gone.
Moonlight shines on my mind and spirit.
It burns across mountainous pain.
It peeks through the struggle to live.
It brightens the darkness of life.

There is a quiet hush in moonlight,
a gentle reflection of memories,
a muted expanse of my future,
a gentle light adorning my life.

In the moonlight of my life,
a gratitude has taken birth
for the gentle hush
of hope in my heart,
and the quiet strength
of my spirit and soul
guided by the light of God.

February 2003

Jerry

His arms and his legs jerked wildly,
slowing his movements and ability to walk.
His speech was so labored that it took patience
and much time to understand what he said.
One thing was abundantly clear though,
because he appeared at my door every day,
"I WANT A JOB!" he would bellow in fury.
He abhorred the sheltered workshop
that had provided him work for years.
"I WANT A JOB!" he would holler,
because it was my job to find employment
for those who were able to work
outside the sheltered workshop.

Knowing Jerry's movements were so slow
in performing any task at hand,
and that his speech was painfully slurred,
and he had a temper lured to work fights,
it seemed quite an impossible task
to find a job outside the workshop,
a sad reality that I had to tell him.

It was my job to find employment
for those able to work for a full day.
I did wish folks had the motivation
that Jerry had, despite a disability
that was so limiting and profound.

Then one day a few months later,
a familiar voice was at my door
"I WANT A JOB!" He loudly bellowed,
having convinced
someone he could work
a full day outside a workshop.

"I WANT A JOB!" he screeched in rage,
pleased to be expecting that I find him a job.
I knew it would take much time,
and a big employment miracle.
We worked months to find an employer
that would let Jerry try a job possibility,
collecting trays that were left on tables
and placing them on a designated stack.

He was one fourth as fast as another worker,
so I thought it unlikely he'd be hired,
until I received a phone call from the employer.
"We'll hire Jerry at the prevailing full wage,"
"he is the first to arrive and the last to leave,
works as hard as he can, enjoys his work,
and never misses a day,
such an example for all our employees,
is worth his weight in gold here,
and certainly is worth a full wage.
We are very glad to have him working,
and he seems glad to be here as well."

I continue to remember Jerry's zeal,
and his motivation to do his best,
inspiring many workers with his effort
to work a full day with exuberance,
allowing no limits to block his way.
If Jerry could have such motivation,
then certainly I could as well,
and if he could allow no limits
to block his way to his dream,
then surely I can do it, also.
He continues to inspire me today
as an example to do my very best.

Such a power exists in motivation,
determination, persistence, and a dream,
believing oneself able to obtain a goal,
though others may have their doubts,
being an example to so many others
of a dream fulfilled despite all odds.
Such power fuels the finest example
that a life could give to our world.

I'll always remember Jerry,
ever bellowing for his dreams.
It keeps me inspired to keep dreaming,
and motivates me to keep trying,
despite all odds and doubts.
It amuses me to have Jerry
as a treasured role model in life,
first to come and last to leave,
seems a wonderful way to live life.

September 2000

Wind

Wind sweeps across desert sand,
making a vast design of waves.
Wind bellows at mountain snow,
making a vast design of soft mounds.
Wind whispers softly through trees,
making a vast design of moving leaves.
Wind caresses a baby's face,
across a vast potential of life.
Without wind is the hush of sound,
creating a vast expanse of calm quiet.

Spirit sweeps across desert life,
making vast designs of wisdom.
Spirit bellows at mountainous pain,
making vast designs of strength.
Spirit caresses a soul's embrace,
making vast the welcome of life.
Without spirit is a hush of soul,
creating a vast expanse of emptiness.

Spirit sweeps across all of existence,
making vast the design of God.
Spirit expands within a soul,
grateful for God's gentle winds.

July 2003

Leslie Anne Miller

Broccoli

Broccoli is a vegetable my husband adores,
though many won't touch the stuff.
He loves to eats it night after night,
till brussel sprouts or asparagus
appear at the store at a discount price.
Only then will he vary from his broccoli.

You'd think his love is probably because
he has a collection of broccoli recipes.
Most assuredly, he does not.
He merely steams the broccoli,
no butter or sauce, no salt or pepper,
and sits down to eat it in a bowl.
A bowl, you howl, does he like it that much?
Most assuredly, he really does.

He eats his broccoli with fresh fish in season,
and his very favorite fish is red snapper.
Oh no, you howl, he eats it every night?
Most assuredly, he does not.
He eats fish almost every night.

He eats broccoli with fish most every night,
and a few variants in season at the right price.
His first love though is broccoli, eaten by the bowl.
Is he an odd duck, in love with his broccoli?
Most assuredly, he really is.

July 2003

Viola

She was an 83-year-old lady,
and an outspoken voice in the community,
although it was a difficult voice to hear.
It was raspy and slurred, soft and hesitant,
yet despite her tiny stature under five feet,
she had a presence that could not be ignored.
She would march up to say her piece,
her head tilted back looking up,
her thick cataract glasses ajar,
and her eyes with a stare of determination.
Always, she wore the same speckled coat,
that was popular several decades past.
Always, her arms had several huge bags
as well as her large bulky purse,
also popular several decades past.

Somehow, with that strong tiny bulk,
and that stern stare of determination,
marching up again to speak her mind,
she was rather like a locomotive
traveling at a threatening speed.
She would screech to a stop abruptly,
uncomfortably close, the better to see,
and have her soft voice promptly heard.
Staring, she would stand very close,
rasping soft about something important,
that needed urgent consideration.
She'd stay there, with that daunting stare,
until she could speak near their ear.
They bent down very close to her mouth,
and only then, she was sure she'd been heard.

Leslie Anne Miller

I have never known such a person
as the Viola I knew decades past,
nor the strength of a tiny personality,
who despite her limits of age, sight, and voice,
always managed to say her piece.
I will always remember little Viola.
She taught me the force of determination,
not diminished by limitation,
but strengthened by personality,
and the sheer will to say her piece,
and make sure that her voice was heard.

November 2003

The Gardener

I know just where to find this man,
my husband on a sunny spring day.
He's usually out planting flowers
or shopping for flowers to plant.

Feeling the depth of his happiness
when outside digging in the dirt,
watering gently his new charges,
checking the leaves for their health,
I like to tease this serious husband,
and ask him if he is again out today
flirting with the flowers and foliage.

There's just one problem that I see
with his love of plants and soil,
and all that he can coax to grow,
he is such an excellent gardener
that things continue to grow
out of control, into each other,
everywhere they shouldn't be.

If I ask this husband of mine,
about his wild gardening power
and the need for pruning sometime,
he just shrugs and smiles and says to me,
"What I'm good at is helping things grow
and I let nature take over from there."
I saw in the reality of overgrown plants
that nature has indeed taken over as
he sternly objects to cutting them back.
I guess I'd rather see the delight in his eyes
than have a trimmed yard and garden outside.
I so love him, which is obvious to neighbors
who watch this wild jungle grow.

November 2003

Leslie Anne Miller

Spider Talk

Oh you poor little spider
what are you doing there
crawling frantically this way and that
and at the bottom of my white bathtub?

No, don't go near the drain
there is no escape down there.
Please crawl near my glass
poised to catch you quick so that
I can take you out to the garden
because that's where you truly belong.

I'll be careful with the glass
not to squash your tiny legs,
you can trust me with this object,
which to you must seem to be
a building that is crashing down,
to squash your very life!

Now that I've caught you in my glass,
out to the garden with you, I'm walking fast.
Good bye now little spider crawling so fast
in my garden where you indeed do belong.

February 2003

Shock

Shattered by trauma, life is far away,
a distant imagined reality, a dream.
The trauma is unbearable, and I cannot see.
I cannot hear and I cannot feel.
I cannot awaken from this nightmare.
Surely, I cannot bear this.
How can I survive this and live?

My mind is clashing symbols, engulfing noise,
it slashes and cuts my soul into pieces.
My screams plead with God that it can't be so.
Come back, my sweetheart, there's a mistake.
Why didn't you take me along with you?
You always have taken me with you before.

The fragments of my being lie scattered.
I am an exhausted and broken soul.
Here I have a choice to make at this moment.
Do I decide to die also, or do I live?

I can begin to start living this moment,
having no idea just how to begin
or how to gather the dust up of my soul.
I decide today to cling to my God,
and trust there is meaning in this dust,
and that God can recreate a new being in me,
a vibrant fresh life of awakening.

I have decided to trust this journey,
separated from my soul mate in this life.
I am alone yet in the process of creating
a purpose that unfolds in this moment,
I feel myself awakening from a nightmare.
I experience myself rising from the dust,
gravely wounded, yet still a special soul,
again choosing to follow God home.

February 2006

Leslie Anne Miller

Joyful Sorrow

I ache for the touch of your hand on my cheek
and long for the warmth of your embrace.
I languish for the strength of your calm glance,
and search for your sweet face amidst the crowd.

The love song in my heart continues with me.
For a time I couldn't hear its soothing sound.
Your presence is conversation in my thoughts,
a consolation amidst the agony of your death.

Still, I reach for your body in the quiet of the night
only to feel the great expanse of your absence.
I imagine the expressions of your dancing face
as your chin and smile and eyes convey joy.

Your spirit is at peace and finding joy there,
and you share your joy and quiet solicitude with me.
Your presence is one of my life's precious gifts
as are memories of our wondrous love song.

My sorrow is a chasm of emotion overwhelming,
at least that is the gulf of loss I'm living.
Yet, today draws close and beckons possibility
of moments joyful, healing and ever changing.
I live today, the joyful sorrow of my reality,
connected yet apart from my beloved spouse.
I'm at peace with our strong love everlasting
today, forever more, and beyond.

March 2006

Lingering

In the quiet of the morning I feel you near me,
though I reach out to touch and you're not here.
When the sun shines on the lofty clouds above,
I know your spirit has found a peaceful home.
Clouds were the poetic symbol of your life.

At dusk, I am embraced by your quiet spirit,
because it was your favorite time of day.
With evening, I live the oneness of our love,
complete with simply feeling you near me.
Late at night, I reach to touch your peace
and feel gratitude for your presence in my life.

I linger with thoughts of your soul nearby
and feel the consolation of quiet peace.
I know one day, I'll leave this life behind,
and connect with you in God's eternal home.
For today, I am grateful for your presence
that gives me strength to live my life another day.

You forever linger in my thoughts and prayers.
We have a love that is forever and beyond.

Linger with me, Love, each moment of today,
as God guides your presence in my world.
I yearn to be with you in heaven's eternal home,
and my yearning gives me courage to fully live.
I know that the love we still share in this life
is but a taste of eternal life with you in God.

May 2007

Joy

I prayed every day for peace, joy, and serenity
in a world without you being there to touch.
It was hard to believe that it would ever happen,
so searing the wound of your untimely death.
I felt great sorrow when life began to heal,
as if feeling good again betrayed your love.

I keep in mind that you always wanted
for me to be happy in life,
and that you are pleased that
today, I can smile now and then.
My tears are still an agony of loss,
but now, they only overwhelm my spirit
now and then, and for a shorter length of time.

It's still new to think of life without you,
so I live life simply, one day at a time.
I cling to God, and my prayer life has deepened.
It brings peace, joy, and serenity to the quiet of my home.
I still look at your wool jacket in the front closet.
I find myself wearing it as my own.
Your ancient adding machine, with its yellowed tape,
still resides proudly on your desk in the study.
I use it to balance my checkbook,
thinking of you treasuring this historic relic,
because, after all, it always continued to work.

I'm amazed to awake in the morning alone,
yet looking forward to what the day might bring.
Your presence is ever near and quite peaceful.
That gives me strength and comfort to live each day.

So love, I choose to go on living my life, fully alive.
I is who I am, and who I will always be.
In prayer, I find the peace, joy, and serenity
that I couldn't imagine in my life without you.
Still, I treasure our conversations in my heart, without words.
They continue to be the foundation of my happiness.
So love, I am out to tend your beloved garden,
and I know that you are happy that I am there,
using the tools that you once held in your hand,
creating a peaceful garden of life, color, and joy.

June 2007

CPSIA information can be obtained
at www.ICGtesting.com
Printed in the USA
FSOW01n1452270315
6044FS

9 780595 492565